To my family – My grandmothers for being eccentric, full of life and so caring. My mother, for encouraging me to follow my own path.

Authenticity is your trademark by Danielle

Dear reader – This book is designed as a guide, to navigate your way through this world by being authentic to who you truly are, it is a little reminder that you are perfect the way you are. This will shine through, once you know your strengths and purpose, then you will be able to walk forward as a leader.

YOUR AUTHENTICITY IS YOUR TRADEMARK

Empowering book for conscientious thinkers and entrepreneurs

By Danielle Christina

www.holisticentrepreneurcoach.com

Synopsis

This book links neuroscience and philosophy with business, and how being a so-called Black Sheep can make great leaders and entrepreneurs. The brain is like the CEO of your body, once activated you can be innovative and make conscious decisions. In today's climate, our brains are either over or under stimulated by the images and information we are receiving from the media. In order to be a conscientious leader, you almost need to be a rebel, to step away from the mainstream conventional lifestyle and create a new lifestyle that is for you. Therefore, feeling more fulfilled in your career choices and business ventures. This book takes it back to basics, reconnecting with your authentic self to be original and set a new trademark that will not only give you purpose but also make you feel more alive by activating the dormant brain cells, using neuro plasticity.

This book outlines the importance of re-programming your mind so you can take steps away from the system and live a life of authenticity – this is your trademark! Each chapter will be dedicated to a Chakra as there are seven chapters that represent each one. As you read and work your way through the book you will be doing the inner work, unblocking (starting from the root Chakra) to find your way back to authenticity.

About the author

Danielle has a Masters in Entrepreneurship and Innovation, from London University. She has also helped manage and had several businesses, her experience ranges from setting up a shop in the high street to mentoring and lecturing at Colleges in the United Kingdom. Danielle is also a trained yoga teacher which has helped her take a more holistic approach to business; she believes that authenticity can help a business thrive.

DEDICATIONS

This book is dedicated to all the Black Sheep that have inspired me throughout my life, the people that never fit in but where they have been brave, courageous and created the unthinkable. Without them life wouldn't be the same. To all the greats and free thinkers; David Bowie, Nelson Mandela, Freddie Mercury, Annie Lennox, Prince, Janis Joplin, Elton John, Princess of Wales, Van Gogh, Tim Walker, Tim Burton, Ann Kenney, Christabel Harriette Pankhurst, Mother Teresa, Martin Luther King, Mahatma Gandhi....

ACKNOWLEDGMENTS

Thank you to my dear friends that have always been my rock, to my childhood friends Katie Binns and David Mackay. To Laura Hills for proofreading this book and being there during these uncertain times. Your support and motivation means the world to me.

TABLE OF CONTENT

FORWARD

In today's culture, entrepreneurs are captivating the media. With TV programmes such as the Apprentice and Dragons Den, we are being inspired by a new generation of people doing things for themselves. It shows that individuals can be successful. With perseverance and talent they are creating businesses that are aligning with their authenticity.

This leads to the question; "Why now, at a time when the world is financially struggling and the recession is looming?" The world has the highest unemployment rate for years and people are being made redundant from work. At this time, you might call it human survival as it is invoking a new generation of entrepreneurs. This culture has given people the drive and determination to set up business.

In 2012 The Creative Boom mentioned that "New survey research released by Dell and StartUp Britain today reveals that Britain's youth has a passion for entrepreneurship. Over 63 percent of students who took part in the survey said that they wanted to start their own business after leaving college or university."

As new budding entrepreneurs are emerging, the creative industry is leading the way. This brings both a creative and business meeting of minds. Creative entrepreneurs are almost prodigies in today's culture. As never before has it been so common that creative individuals are bringing business to their art.

"Entrepreneurs in the creative economy...operate like Say's original model entrepreneur but with an important difference...they use creativity to unlock the wealth that lies within themselves. Like true capitalists, they believe that this creative wealth, if managed right, will engender more wealth."[1]

Entrepreneurs in the creative industry needs to have the knowledge of the creative aspects of business. Understanding the industry inside-out in order to succeed at business. As the competition is so high, every entrepreneur needs to know the market, customers and planning. In order to produce products that will sell and make profit in business.

"These people instinctively think for themselves, instinctively network, instinctively keep several balls in the air at once. They are the shock troops not only for new ideas about our culture but for new ideas about working in it." John Howkins, 2001.

It's only in the past century that creative entrepreneurs have been given the recognition from society (as before it was mostly academics that where high earners). Proving that a creative person can turn their creation into a product that makes money. Like Howkins implied, creative entrepreneurs are good at multi-tasking. They need to know every area of the business from the start of creation to the final sell.

---

[1] John Howkins, The Creative Economy: How to Make Money from Ideas, 2001

Now with recognition, creative entrepreneurs can thrive and constantly prosper in society. Creating new products that not only captivate the consumer, enduring business through aligning with their authenticity.

INTRODUCTION

"Differentiation is one of the most important strategic and tactical activities in which companies must constantly engage."- Theodore Levitt

After completing my Master's in Entrepreneurship and Innovation several years ago, I have worked with a variety of businesses, and lectured at colleges. Feeling compelled to work with start-up entrepreneurs to give them confidence and the skills required in business, I have worked with many brands, designers, entrepreneurs, and coaches. One thing I noticed is how many people are frightened of failure or judgment, to the point that sometimes they totally give up or don't start. The external world really affects their internal monologue. Even if they are aware of their skills and know they are capable, they resist the change. Why? Because we have to leave the comfort zone to be able to create something new. And for many this can be daunting and overwhelming. It takes courage and accountability to start a new project or business.

I have not always been business savvy, I first graduated from University in design and my dream was to be a fashion designer (now I have my own fashion yoga brand). So, I worked for several fashion magazines and design houses before realising that I wanted to be my own boss. While I was contemplating this idea, ironically, I got made redundant from my job. This forced me to take the leap (I think this was the Universe guiding me). I wanted to create my own rules and expel my creativity. So, I decided to enrol in an MA business program in London, to become business savvy. This then gave me the business skills in order to create my own.

However, it doesn't end there. Shortly after completing my MA, my romantic relationship ended, I had to move out of my apartment, and I got made redundant again (because I didn't listen the first time). As you can imagine, my stress levels were through the roof, I had no idea what I was going to do or where I was going to go. So, I started practising yoga, to maintain my sanity. After seeing the benefits in only a few weeks and reading all the books imaginable, I decided to enrol in a yoga teacher training course. I wanted to gain a deeper understanding of the philosophy and the mind, body connection. This generated the idea of holistic business, giving individuals the confidence to create a business that aligns with their authenticity.

This book helps define your authenticity and find your unique selling point by using the Black Sheep mindset concept. This is a concept I created, to help separate you from the crowd, so you can live a lifestyle and build a business from your authenticity – and in turn this will become your trademark.

In today's society (in the book I call this the Manmade Reality Scape), it is increasingly necessary that we make conscientious decisions and actions. That we move forward with consciousness and courage. That we are proactive, instead of reactive. Taking action steps that align internally, rather than what is being projected externally. In today's society we have been conditioned to control every aspect of our life, that we have to make things happen to feel rewarded and fit into the system. We get told what we should do and how we should look by projectivisation, and we get so caught up in this that we lose our sense of self and authenticity. Making decisions and taking actions from a place of insecurity, because that is what we have been told to do, rather than what we want to do and aligns with us.

The Black Sheep mindset requires us to have a strong foundation of sense of self, for confidence to make change happen. If we are going to be leaders or innovative entrepreneurs then we need to think outside the box, by creating something new and unique. We can do this by examining and creating strong neuron pathways using neuroplasticity. With neuroplasticity, we can change our mindset and behavioural patterns that we have been conditioned (to have by society or cultural). Therefore, gaining confidence and becoming more aligned with our authenticity.

Throughout this book I use the seven Chakras to realign us back to our sense of self and consciousness. To regain confidence and safety in being ourselves, by knowing that we are whole and complete beings. This will help stabilise our nervous system so we don't make fear based decisions and create stronger self-confidence.

Therefore, we will be able to break patterns of behaviour that no longer serve our mission and be able to make conscientious choices that serve our lifestyle and business.

CHAPTER ONE:

BE THE BLACK SHEEP
MULADHARA CHAKRA

"In a society that profits from self-doubt, liking yourself is a rebellious act" – Caroline Caldwell

Throughout this book I will be talking about the Black Sheep mindset. This doesn't necessarily mean that you have to be a Black Sheep, however it will help you adopt the mindset so you can make conscientious and authentic lifestyle choices and business decisions. What does a Black Sheep mindset refer to? It refers to being rebellious in a society that tells you how to act, so you take consciousness actions that align with your authenticity (sense of self). Which will ultimately make you feel more aligned and fulfilled in both your decision making and actions; becoming more proactive than reactive by reprogramming our neuron pathways.

Whereas, some of you might already feel like a Black Sheep; the Black Sheep are normally set apart from the crowd, because they choose not to compromise their morals, values or character. Therefore, they normally look or act different from their peers, often being labelled as alternative. The Black Sheep seek those that hold the same standards and consciousness as themselves. These people normally make great leaders because they are resilient and courageous (you have to be both of these not to follow the crowd). Have you ever felt like you don't fit in? The truth is, most of us feel this way a little.

I have always felt like a Black Sheep and had a little rebel in me, not in a mischievous way but with a sense of wonder and freedom. When I was younger, I remember dancing everywhere, even at school. I would often get told off for not paying enough attention in class and not conforming. Later I realised that this was simply because they didn't capture my attention. I found school to be rather tactile, regimented, and mind-numbing. I was always asking questions (I must have drove my primary school teachers mad). I questioned everything, the teachings, and the system just because I was curious and wanted to understand the reasons behind doing things. I didn't feel like it left enough room for growth or expansion, instead it was a rule book we must follow to gain points (or gold stars at that age) and this simply didn't interest me. I didn't want or need this instant gratification that the system wanted me to play into.

Living in today's society (system), we have all been conditioned to live a certain lifestyle. Those that don't conform or choose a different path are looked down upon and this is exactly the reason why so many continue the cycle, afraid to step out, take the leap and make conscientious actions.

It is not that we can't be different, we all have the potential to live life to the fullest; it is the fact that if we do so then we fear we will be made an outcast from society and rejected from a system that we have been born into. Therefore we carry on conforming, living and working in the system. Doing, instead of feeling and being, we have become disconnected to our true selves and authenticity, to fit into the system and to be accepted. In order to have the job title, get the qualification, buy a house etc we have to work 8 hours per 365 days per year, in a job just to pay the bills, buy the house and the fancy car. Working more than living (with only 24 days holiday). While this lifestyle is considered the norm in the current system, it is important to ask who are you doing this for? And do we all need to live the same lifestyle (educational system, job, marry, children and then death)? What about the space in between all this, are you leaving yourself enough space to live and be your authentic self? To follow your passion, your dreams and do what makes you feel alive?

MANMADE REALITY SCAPE

In this book I will make references to the system or society we live in, I call this the Manmade Reality Scape. I am not suggesting that all systems are malicious, they are fundamental and can create productivity (which I will talk about later in the book). However, we need to identify how they can work for us so we can make conscious decisions and maintain our authenticity.

One of the reasons we have such little self-worth, love and good mental health is because we have all experienced the pressure of social conditioning to fit into the system. Where we feel like we 'should' fit in, to look a certain way to be accepted and loved, to have the good career with status so we are respected by our peers. But who gave us this conditioning, where did these ideas come from? Government, media, culture, society, religion, and our parents. This way of thinking has been passed down from generation to generation, the regularity of it has made it normal. We grow up believing we must fit into certain boxes in order to be accepted. However, the most ironic thing is, the more we try to fit into a certain role or group, the more we become less ourselves and forget all we need to do is simply BE. We are not humans-doing, we are human beings! The more we try to fit into the mould the more we distort our true nature (ourselves), lose our authenticity and our true sense of reality.

We are brought into the world with a lot of 'shoulds' which misshapes our sense of self. Here are some 'shoulds' that we have been told in life:

- You should look a certain way
- You should go to this University to get good career
- You should have that job
- You should feel this way
- You should marry this type of person

Do any of these sound familiar to you? The thing is, we often feel like we are behind in life or not good enough because we are trying to keep up with all the 'shoulds' that society has conditioned us to think we need but this thought process only holds us back.

Those of us that have experienced city life, probably at some point felt a part of the 'Rat Race'. The repetitive everyday cycle to try and get ahead financially which is exhausting. It is the constant need to improve, compete, which means working harder, faster and longer hours. Leaving many drained and de-valued, losing self-morale. The term 'selling your soul to the devil' comes to mind, a metaphor for losing your own soul. If we are in a constant state of giving and trying to fit into the system, then we lose our soul and authenticity. We begin to live from a place of repetitive behaviour, like robots. Not giving ourselves time or space to step back, breathe and ask questions. Like why am I doing this and what am I doing it for?

Rat Race = "The term referring to rats attempting to earn a reward such as cheese, in vain"

The most ironic thing is, we think the harder we work, the more we will impress and achieve. But have you ever been in a job where you are working so hard but your efforts have not been recognised? Have you felt like your promotion should come any day but it never does? Have you ever felt that your colleagues are fighting to be seen for the promotion? I have! This is not a healthy place to be, this kind of environment can literally destroy your health and self-esteem. The exhaustion from being in this kind of environment can break down your immune system. Therefore, there is increasingly depression and mental health breakdown in the Western World. This system needs to be questioned. We humans need to be in a productive environment that builds on our self-worth and esteem, not deplete it. So, we can grow, develop, evolve and expand. However, we get caught up in the system and repeat the daily cycle, in the depleting environment.

The Manmade Reality Scape that the majority of us live in, consists of economical systems, social order and role of state. The social order means that governments and corporations have set up systems to create order in society. So the population can feel safe and society can run effectively. For example, we have shopping centres and food markets where we can go to buy food. While these serve a purpose and generally make our lives a lot easier to function, they also create a rigged system that consumes us (this is where the word 'consumer' comes from, we are not only told what to buy but also what information to consume and how we should live).

It is natural for us humans to easily fall into repetitive patterns of behaviour because we feel safe doing what we know to be true. The ego is the part of the mind where our self-doubt comes in because its aim is the basic survival action, to keep us safe and protect us. So, we convince ourselves that change is not safe, and being in our comfort zone is much safer. Whether we like it or not, we keep repeating the same patterns and routines because they have become normalised to us. Our brain tricks us into thinking these patterns are safe, so we continue to do them. It is not until we start to question things, that we can break the mould, routine and patterns, to start to make conscious actions. This is why we need to question the established systems that are in place and ask if they serve us on a personal level. This book will help explore what serves the individual and how we can make decisions and lead a life through our authenticity.

QUESTION YOUR REALITY

This comes to my second point; how important it is to ask questions! We have been conditioned so deeply that we believe we are being disobedient, rebellious (or worse, a failure) if we choose a different path. We fear of becoming the Black Sheep; but let me tell you something, the Black Sheep are brilliant! They are the innovators, the creators, the spiritual, the leaders. Why? Because nothing NEW ever came from normal or comfort zones. Innovators, creators, leader all have one quality in common, the ability to take a different path, break the mould and think outside of the box. That one quality is courage; and using it to question their reality and execute a new one.

"Whatever you decide to do in life, make sure you do it from a place of love, freedom and self-respect. Don't act in fear or one day you will look back on life and feel like you haven't lived."

I remember when I was younger, I got pulled up in class by my teacher, he said "Danielle, you ask a lot of questions!"

Me: Ironically, I replied with another question, asking "is that a bad thing?"

Teacher: My teacher thought for a second and then replied saying, "no, it actually a really good thing. It means that you are interested in the subject and want to understand, learn and develop."

This was one of my favourite teachers because he was willing to take a step back for the greater good and think outside the box. He was not condescending or patronising, like all good teachers he put the students' needs first, before the rule book.

"A good teacher is always a student!"

It is only when we let our ego become the better of us that we become stubborn, think we know it all, stop learning and therefore developing. As I mentioned before, the ego comes from a place of fear, creating self-doubt, judgment, and disconnection, in order to protect us and keep us safe (keeping us in the comfort zone). So believing you already know everything, actually is counterproductive and probably means you know very little because you stopped developing and only know your 'version of reality.'

If we want to grasp the full version of reality then we need to experience new things, new cultures and different ways of thinking. To be constantly learning in order to develop and expand and gain more knowledge of the world.

Duncan Wardle was the former head of Innovation & Creativity at Disney and founder of ID8 and Innov8. His job is to help enterprise think outside the box, therefore being more innovative and creative. He suggests the best way to do this is by asking the right questions that form your reality. In 2018 Wardle spoke at a Ted Talk, stating that the most innovative projects of the 21st century started by asking questions, this allows us to open our mind to what we know so we can form new opinions and generate new way of doing things. Demonstrating that, two groups of colleagues were given a task to come up with a new idea, however one group had a stranger. Although the group with the stranger felt a little uncomfortable with someone new in the group, they won the challenge because the stranger gave them a new perspective, he challenged the way the colleagues previously did things so the group created something new.

Likewise, Dr Robert Anthony has spent most of his life work dedicated to helping people question their reality. He has a PHD in cognitive psychology and masters in Neurolinguistics. He suggests that we all have the capability to live life on our terms if we become aware of our surroundings and question our reality (challenging where our thoughts and behaviour come from). He is a big advocator for living in your authenticity and not conforming to social or culture conditions, quoting "The opposite of bravery is not cowardice but conformity".

Asking more questions creates greater understanding which leads to more empathy and self-development. Think outside your reality (box, bubble) and break your mould. This will lead to knowing yourself, feeling happier and healthier and becoming more innovative and creative. All good things happen when we start to question the system and break free. This concept requires a lot of courage and persistence because there is no quick fix, however we can start by asking questions. Why do I feel this way? Why do I act that way? Once we can analyse our reality, we can start to shift our thought process into a choice of action, rather than reaction.

MULADHARA CHAKRA

As we read through the book, each chapter will be related to one of the seven chakras, so we can do the internal work which will help us connected to our authenticity. In yoga we often talk about the seven chakras, these are energy points running through the body representing different aspects of ourselves. Sometimes, these energy points get blocked so we are unable to function fully in these areas. However, when they are open, then we can be in a state of flow and alignment. This means our energy is balanced and can function at its full potential.

Muladara is the first in the sequences and represents the root, base or foundation, it is the anchored in reality (as we know it). It is placed at the base of the spine (near the sitting bones). It Symbolises the Lotus flower. The flower has to grow up through the muddy water, in order to bloom. This is the seed or root; it is considered the foundation of the 'energy body'. The idea being, 'what you sow, you will reap'. Being rooted and grounded in an environment that allows you to flourish and grow. Which suggests picking the right environment for your life by questioning your reality, in order for positive growth, development and expansion. One of the four petals of the flower symbol represents Dharma. Dharma means your soul purpose. So being in the right environment will allow you to flourish and live in your soul purpose. This is a reminder to question our reality, to see if the system we individually are living in, is the right environment for us to grow, flourish and live a life of fulfilment.

When in balance, we feel grounded, anchored, secure, safe and present. It represents our basic survival needs, like, water, food, home or the sense of security that a home brings. As it is based at the base of the spine, it holds the foundation of the body and responsible for the functioning of the lower part of the body. Such as the Bladder, Kidneys and Lower Back, which is where the adrenalin glades are located. The adrenaline glades produce adrenalin and stimulate our nervous system, flight or fight response. So when in balance, our nervous system is in a state of homeostasis self-regulation and we feel safe, being able to make decisions from a place of security. When out of balance we feel unsafe, this is when we react, either in fight or flight mode, because out sympathetic nervous system has been activated. This can appear as many emotional and physical forms, either underactive or overactive symptoms.

Root Chakra imbalance Symptoms:

Overactive Symptoms	Underactive Symptoms
Feeling Materialistic	Insecure and Fearful
Feeling Greedy	Indecisive
Impulsive	Low self-confidence
Aggressive	Restlessness or Anxious
Difficulty accepting change	Stressed
	Feeling lack of security with money or basic survival needs

These can take on physical symptoms, which are normally located in the lower part of the body. For example, the Kidney stones, Bladder problems, lower back pain, constipation or diarrhoea and eating disorders or obesity.

The aim, of course is to get the balance between the overactive and underactive. When in balance we will have more energy to perform tasks, be able to make decisions and fundamentally feel secure. In order to do this we must maintain a health environment, one which we can feel safe and nurtured. Alongside trusting ourselves. If we trust ourselves, then we will be more confident in our decision making, knowing that we can lean on ourselves to survive in the world. This means, practising critical thinking – Is my reality supporting me? Once you establish what works for you and what does not, then you can start to make changes towards what works for you. It is not about staying in your comfort zone to feel safe but questioning it. It is about exploring and moving beyond your comfort zone into a place where you can feel safe to be yourself. When this chakra is fully aligned, we will feel safe within ourselves, trusting ourselves, making decisions and taking action steps that align with who we are.

EXCERCISE 1: QUESTIONING YOUR REALITY

Let's take a moment to think about everything in chapter one; questioning your reality. Now I want you to write a list of everything you have been told that you should do, next to it, simply write if you wanted to do it or not. After you have done this, you will identify how many things are your decisions and how many things are decisions of others?

What have I been told to do? Or feel you should do?	Did I want to do it? (be honest)	Did I do it?	If so, was it beneficial?

If you did the things in the first column but you didn't want to then work through the next few chapters to discover how to change your neuro pathways so you can make more decisions based on your authenticity. If you decided not to do the things in the first column because you felt they didn't align with you then you have the ability to question your reality and make conscious decisions. This can differ depending on the subject matter, some of us might feel more confident in some areas of our lives then other area, however this exercise will outline what areas they are (romance, career, self-image etc.).

Notes:

CHAPTER TWO:

JUMPING THE FENCE

SACRAL CHAKRA

Once we acknowledge our own reality and decide to make the step towards living a life of fulfilment and authenticity. Then we need to work on our own inner strength to break the mould and jump the fence.

This chapter is dedicated to authenticity, allowing space for you to be yourself and connect with your sense of self. Creating self-awareness so you feel comfortable in your own skin to take the leap to jump the fence, break free from the herd and find your own path. With a sense of self-worth and confidence we can gain the courage to build a new way of life for ourselves and create the business from our essence.

This is going to take courage, drive and persistence. Because breaking the mould is almost like having an addiction. We are so addicted to this way of life, that it is not going to be easy. There will be a lot of self-doubt, so we need to do the inner work to build on self-confidence. Patterns are hard to break, simply because we are used to doing them, they are familiar and safe. So we get into a repetitive cycle. The thought of doing something new, can be a challenge and overwhelming because we are coming out of our comfort zone.

As we discovered, the first step is to question your own reality. The next step is to decide your next move and make your own decisions. To take conscious action steps to create a new story for yourself.

UNIQUE SELLING POINT

When you honour yourself and act from a place of authenticity to create something new, then you are being original, one of a kind. This sets you apart from your competitors in an over saturated market and focuses on your Unique Selling Point (USP). Your journey, personality, and service makes you individual, it makes you unique. In order to stand out from the crowd (flock of sheep), you simply just need to be in-tune with who you really are. Instead of following the crowd, set yourself apart from it. The USP strategy was formed as part of the business model canvas in the 1940s. It is the benefit that distinguishes you or your offer apart from your competitors in the marketplace. But it order to do this, you need to dig deep into your sense of self, to truly know yourself and what aligns with you. Once you can identify with your authentic self, then you can distinguish what sets you apart from others, this will become your trademark, your stamp on the world.

SENSE OF SELF

In order to jump the fence and stop following the herd/crowd we need to follow our own intuition and connect to our authentic self. How do we connect to our sense of self? It is said that an infant develops their sense of self within the first year of life, brain development occurs between 18-24 months of age. And neuroscientists suggest that brain functions are adapted to the social construction and environment that we experience within these years. Neural basis of self is the idea of using neuroscience to understand the biological process of what happens in the brain to form our perceptions of self. We are biologically driven and compelled by our neural drives.

We know that the right side of the brain is more active and dominant in the first year of life, neuroscientists re-named this as the 'right mind'. Suggesting it is the right way to think; the right side of the brain is related to our emotions, intuition, empathy, creativity and understanding. For the first few years this is all we know and do, is to feel and act upon our emotions. We listen to that 'gut feeling' and act on what feels right for us. If we feel hungry, tired, joyful we express these though our emotions. Either by crying or laughing. Life is pretty simple, there is no hidden motive or ego, if we want or need something, we express it. We act in innocence and this is our true essence and authentic self. It is only later, moving more into adulthood that the left side of the brain is more prominent (planning and logic).

As most infants spend most of their early years of life with their mother, they start to imitate her reactions, expressions and emotions to the world. Creating an interpersonal channel of synchronicity. Providing evidence that in the early years of life we are more focused on the right side of the brain (the feminine emotions and intuition), alongside developing our sense of self. It is when our neuro pathways are formed, expressing how we relate to the world and we are our most authentic self (we are more in tunned to our wants and needs). At this stage we have not formed any boundaries, we are completely open and accepting.

ATTACHMENT THEAORY

Attachment Theory explains how we develop our sense of self in the early years of life, it is a psychological and ethological concept, concerning relationships between people and the way we develop as individuals. The theory was formed by the psychoanalyst, John Bowlby. Suggesting that in the early years of life were infants build relations with their consistent caregivers. Connections are formed between the infant (between six months to two years old) and the caregiver (often a parent). Attachment is developed as a form of security. As the caregiver is meant to protect us and make us feel secure (if the caregiver is fully functioning). We rely on our caregiver to teach us basic survival skills, such as feeding us when we feel hunger, dressing us for warmth and protecting us from and hazards, fundamentally they are meant to show love and care. So, we know we are safe and secure, therefore developing self-confidence. The idea of safety builds trust; trust in others and in one's self.

As the attachment is formed between the infant and caregiver so is the idea of safety and security, therefore we start to absorb our caregivers principles and values. Because we trust the caregiver with our fundamental survival, we start to trust them in other areas in life, and how they view the world. As we grow, we take on our caregivers view of the world, this is often shown in how be react and behave in certain situations in life; it is related to our personal values and moral structure that we relate to.

This is where a part of believe systems and cultural conditioning is formed, if the caregivers believes an individual should be educated then we also absorb this belief. This is the same as religion, politics, and social relations. For example, if an infant is brought up in a religious environment then they will perceive this to be true. It is only when we are fully functioning adults that we can make our own analogy of what we believe to be true, creating our own values and ideals. However, because the bond is so strong between the caregiver and individual in the early years of life, we often maintain the same views, beliefs and actions. It takes a very strong character to become fully independent, creating their own belief system that is not attached to the caregivers.

If the caregiver shows unconditional love and safety, then the individual is more likely to become independent and make their own life decisions because they know they are supported to do so. Our nervous system is balanced and in a state of homeostasis, creating a sense of safety and security without attachment. Homeostasis is the name given for a steady internal, physical, and chemical condition for optimal functioning individuals (humans). It is only when we feel unsafe that our nervous system becomes imbalanced, that we either go into a fight or flight mode reaction because our sympathetic nervous system is activated or become submissive with an overreacting parasympathetic nervous system. So the key is to know that we are safe and loved enough to make our own life decisions and think for ourselves (however, this is not always as simple because most of us have an attachment to our caregivers in some shape or form because our caregivers are just humans navigating their way through life too and trying to do the best they can. Some better than others. This just means there might be healing work to be done).

This is why, it is the oldest child (or last child with extreme age gap between siblings), that often feels like the Black Sheep because they are the first in the generations to go out into the world, to find their way (lead the way). They don't have someone to guide them,

ABSOLUTE TRUTH V THEORY OF MIND

To really gain a deeper understanding of sense of self, then we need to grasp these two theories, to understand which one is our authentic self and which one is projected. The theory of the mind was developed in 1600s by John Locke, this challenged the idea of the Absolutism. Locke was an English philosopher and physician, known as the father of Liberalism and Enlightenment thinker's movement. His theory of mind is often cited as the original concept of identity and self. Identifying the idea of self and consciousness. His work was revolutionary, it defied the status-quo at the time, which was Absolutism. Absolutism Truth was a theory formed by politicians and clerical powers. This was the foundation of society and culture as we know it today. Absolutism Truth is a theory based upon the idea that reality in fixed and inflexible structures (coinciding with the Left side of the brain characteristics, of logic, planning and structure), it is regimented and unaltered. This theory highlights objects that are 'true', for example, a wall is a wall. It examines what we can see and touch right in front of us. Whereas the Theory of Mind examines beyond the physical objectification and looks at consciousness. Leaving space for critical thinking, provoking people to think for themselves and have their own opinion on how they view the world. Rather than being told what they see as true.

"New opinions are always suspected, and usually opposed, without any reason but because they are not common" – John Locke

Of course, the patriarchy and clerical establishment didn't like the concept of Theory of Mind because it allowed people to make their own decisions, rather than being told what is right or wrong. Which allows for more freedom and liberation, rather than control and tyranny.

Consciousness promotes the idea for people to become independent and in tune to what they believe to be true, trusting in their own intuition. Most importantly it allows each person to have different ideas that resonates with the individual, being authentic to themselves, rather than what they think they 'should' or 'shouldn't' do.

When I was younger, I had 1:1 tuition with an English teacher to improve my reading and writing. She would ask me, "how do you think this word should be spelt?" Instead of automatically responding with what I thought, I would sit there thinking what the right answer was. I didn't want to say something that was wrong so I said nothing at all. And when I did reply, my answer was wrong because I didn't go with my 'gut feeling', speak my truth; instead, I said what I thought my teacher wanted to hear. I was lacking a lot of confidence in this area (which is why this book is such a miracle). I was so consumed by pleasing other people that I neglected my own opinions and thoughts. Which ironically led me to say the wrong answer (if I trusted my gut then I would have said the right thing).

This being said, Locke suggests that being aware, awake and conscientious is liberating. When we can conceive our own ideals and reasoning, it creates free thinking and decision making. We are able to choose! Having the ability to choose creates self-awareness and builds on our identity of self. Meaning we become more individual in our own entity, rather than following rules and regulations created for the masses.

However, it is important to create balance between Absolute Truth and Theory of Mind, by acknowledging what is and accepting it but also be conscious so we can make our own decisions and not be afraid to express them, to speak our truth. It is good to take an objectified view of the world, to look at a situation for what it is and not label it as good or bad. To honour your feelings surrounding the situation, without labelling them as good or bad. We often categorise emotions and actions as good or bad, putting labels on things and people in boxes. This often creates anxiety, stress and judgment (crying is seen as negative, however if we just accept it as an emotion without the label there is less judgment and more freedom of expression, allowing us to be authentic). This only creates judgment and where there is judgment, there is separation. To be authentic we need to connect, not to feel separate from oneself. Building confidence to make decisions and take actions that align with who we are.

INTUITION

Learning to lean on your own intuition can be a force that sets us free and away to adopt the Black Sheep mindset. When we trust our own choices and decisions (rather than being told from outside forces), we are more inclined to feel happier and more fulfilled. Why? Because it stimulates the brain. When our mind is active, it is stimulated so you will naturally feel more alive and good. Leaning on your own intuition will stimulate your brain, creating dopamine (the positive chemical).

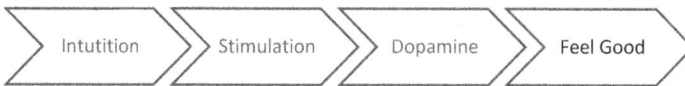

Intutition 〉 Stimulation 〉 Dopamine 〉 Feel Good

Stimulation = To rouse action. It creates dopamine in the brain which makes you feel good and what motivates you. Dopamine provides your zest for life! There are about 86 billion neurons in the human brain that communicate with each other, via brain chemicals, called neurotransmitters. Dopamine can be triggered by body or brain stimulation. Therefore, being able to make a critical decision by following our intuition can stimulate the brain and produce dopamine, which make us feel motivated. Therefore, creating your own path and decision making, gives us a lust for life!

Left Side of Brain	Right side of Brain
Structure	Fluid/Adaptable
Logic/Realism	Imagination
Strategy	Creativity
Planning	Intuition

We have two side of the brain, left and right. When the right side of the brain isn't functioning or in motion, it can think we are literally DEAD. So the more we don't think for ourselves, the more numb, restricted and dead we feel. Which is why so many people feel depressed in today's culture. The more we think for ourselves, following our intuition, the more alive, expansive and motivated we feel. This is because of the signals that are being sent to the brain.

In today's Manmade Reality Scape we use the left side of the brain 80% of the time, this is the side we do our planning and logical thinking. The right side of the brain is where we store our creativity, authenticity and intuition. We use the left side in our daily routine and at work. Our culture has learnt to focus and dependant on this side of the brain, however the right side has been neglected. The right side of the brain is equally important (some would say more important). We need both in order to be a fully functional human.

However, we often concentrate on the left side because this is what we have been conditioned to believe is more important by society and social system. But this couldn't be further from the truth. We are meant to lean on the right side of the brain first and then use the left side to make it happen. For example, 1) creating something new or innovative and then using a strategy and planning to bring it to life. 2) Following your intuition which tells you what decision to make and then implementing it in a logical way.

"This is the recipe for success, activating your authenticity and intuition (right side of brain), then implementing strategy and planning (left side of brain)."

The reason we have lost connection to the right side of the brain, that activates our authenticity is because we have been told to 'follow'. How often have you heard the phrase, "Do as I say" or "Stop day-dreaming" or "Be logical". It is frowned upon to use the right side of the brain. Almost dismissing it like it is not important or intelligent. However, you need to be extremely clever to create something new.

- Scientists use the right side of their brain to create new medicine
- Mathematicians use the right side of their brain to create a new equation
- Artists use the right side of the brain to create a masterpiece

The fact is the less we use the right side of the brain, the less likely we are to think for ourselves and in tune with our intuition. Which means we are more likely to take orders and start to feel numb.

WHAT DOES SUCCESS MEAN?

We all define success differently, a part of the way we define success depends on the type of environment we have been brought up in. In this book I define success as being authentic and creating a lifestyle that represents that, ultimately a lifestyle that makes you happy. Many other books define success as being rich and rooted in money and consumption, but does money really bring happiness? No. This is not a get rich quick book because the only reason one seeks money is to ultimately feel happy, that is the end goal. Money is an external part of the equation, not the end result. However, if we focus on our mindset and neuropathways, then we can create happiness, this is what this book refers to as successful. It is an internal process to live in our authenticity.

I find it so inspirational when I find out successful people's back story (people living in their authenticity). Their life might look perfect now and they might seem like they have it all figured out. However, their back story explains all their trials and tribulations, that they had to go through to get where they are now. Almost every inspiring person I know has had a breaking point where they had to re-evaluate their life. This breaking point actually helped them to create a new life. They have broken away old patterns or structures in their life that were no longer serving their greater good (bad habits, dysfunctional relationships etc). The breaking point gave them two choices and it made them decide. To either completely fall apart or make the change. And of course, they chose to make the change.

We were born to survive; our bodies and ego are working for us. We just need to listen to our bodies (what we need) and our intuition.

SACRAL CHAKRA

The Sacral chakra is associated with sense of self and where we feel most alive, by connection to our five senses. It is the second chakra in the sequence, located above the pubic bone and below the navel and encompasses the general region and the hypogastric plexus. Its traditional name is called Svadhishthana. The word Svadhishthana is translated and means **"the dwelling place of the self"**. It represents vitality and sexual energy as birthing is as sign of creation and new life. Meaning connection to one's authenticity, sense of self and starting point to the individual life force. This can be interpreted in the physical and the spiritual form. For example, giving birth is a physical action, but our sense of self is spiritual. It is where our soul and body are created.

If is highly important to connect with your body, creating a mind body balance. When we connect with our body, we feel embodied. This activates our sense of self, making us feel more present and alive. It is where our physical and emotional body meets.

This Chakra will become balanced when we do things that makes us feel alive and give us pleasure. This can be sexual, self-pleasure, exercising, anything that requires physical activity. For example, going for a run will get your blood circulation working, moving oxygen around your body through your red blood cells. Once this reaches your muscles, you will have more energy and your brain will be activated. Creating the happy chemicals in your body, serotonin which is also a classified as a neurotransmitter. Sending happy hormones around your body. The more movement the body does, the more these chemicals will be released, resulting in creating a feeling of being good to be alive.

The opposite to this is being depressed, the sense of not feeling good to be alive. This often occurs when we are stagnant, when we experience no movement or pleasure. We start to feel disconnected to our body and sense of self. This can have many symptoms, showing up as problems with the kidneys and reproductive organs. Such as urinary infections, stiffness and low in energy.

Symptoms of out of balanced Sacral Chakra looks like:

Overactive	Underactive
Depression	Lack of creativity and passion
Hypersensitive and over emotional	Feeling unemotional
Having trouble connecting with others, being cold	Comparing yourself to others, self-judgment
Struggle to deal with change	Low libido

The Sacral Chakra represents the colour orange, therefore if you eat orange food and wear orange, it will help balance this area. Think about eating salmon, orange fruit and vegetables. Maintaining a healthy energy point in this area will consist of being physically active and doing things that your are passionate about or expressing yourself through our body (like being creative, dancing, singing, running). This will help connect with your body and sense of self.

EXERCISE 2: CONNECTING TO SENSE OF SELF

Chant **I AM**. These are two of the most powerful words because what you put after them shapes your reality; use it as an affirmation or mantra. This exercise will empower you as the words 'I am' are so powerful in themselves because they draw your attention inwards and create a sense of being alive and present. As you chant it will start to activate your neuro pathways.

Combine this by connecting to your body through your breath (your life force), sit in any meditative pose with your spine erect. Then draw attention to where the Sacral Chakra is located and engage your pelvic floor, lower tip of spine and genitals. Take deep slow breaths, on the inhale, take you breath all the way down and then fully exhale. The process will help you reconnect inwardly, connecting to your sense of self.

CHAPTER THREE:

GROWING YOUR OWN GRASS
SOLAR PLEXUS

As we have discovered, conscious thinking and decision making stimulates the brain and senses. So connecting to your authenticity and intuition is necessary to feel motivated.

So what's next, after you have broken away from the old system that was not serving you mentally or physically, and decided to create a new life for yourself? Once you have jumped the fence (chapter two), then you need to learn to grow your own grass, to lay a new path and foundation for growth. Like the age old saying, "energy flows where your attention and focus goes" – this might sound obvious but it is so true! Where you put your time and energy, you will develop and grow in that area. Your mindset is the key for setting the foundation to your new life.

"The grass is always greener where you water it"

NEUROSCIENCE

Before we talk about mindset, it's important to understand how the brain works; neuro plasticity suggests that our brain neural network changes through growth and reorganisation. Neural networks in the brain are what form our understanding of the world and how we function in everyday life. Neural plasticity suggests these networks can be changed. These changes range from individual neurons making new connections in the brain, to systematic adjustments like cortical re-mapping. This means our brains have the ability to change. For example – Learning something new, taking on a new activity, environmental influences or psychological stress all play important part in creating new neuro pathways in your brain.

"Neuroplasticity was once thought by neuroscientists to manifest only during childhood, but research in the later half of the 20th century showed that many aspects of the brain exhibiting a higher degree of plasticity were in the adult brain" – (Brain Mechanisms in Conditioning and Learning, Livingston RB, 1966).

This being said, it suggests that the adult brain is not entirely hard wired, with fixed neuronal circuits. There is evidence that neurogenesis occurs in the adult brain and such changes can persist well into old age (Neurogenesis in the adult primate neocortex: an evaluation of the evidence, Rakic P, 2002). With training we have the ability to change the way we act and think, by using cognitive training techniques and other methods. This evidence suggests that we can be innovative, creative and make life changes throughout adult life. [Disclaimer - So even if you do not think of yourself as a creative person, you can be]

MINDSET

Mindset is the key to not only following your dreams but achieving them. With a 'can do' attitude, you are more likely to build and maintain the life you want and a business that thrives.

To be able to achieve a healthy mindset, you need hope. Hope will stop you from giving up and pursuing your goals. With a hopeful mindset you will believe you have a brighter future and this will motivate you to achieve it. You need to believe in your future life/business so you are not fighting with the current to achieve it but flowing with it, believe that everything is working in your favour. This does not mean sit back and don't do anything, you still need to work towards your goals. However, it does mean that we can let go of any worry or anxiety surrounding starting something new.

Mindset = a habitual or characteristic mental attitude which determines how you will interpret and respond to situations

There are two different types of mindsets; fixed and growth. People with a 'fixed' mindset believe their qualities are unchangeable, in-born and fixed. However, people with a 'growth' mindset believe they can change, their abilities can be develop and progress through hard work and determination. Carol Dweckis a Stanford psychologist, she suggests that many people are trained in the two types of mindsets early in life, often through the way they are raised or their experiences in school. Certain characteristics can be assigned to either a fixed or growth mindset (Carol Dweck www.verywellmind.com, March 02. 2020)

Fixed Mindsets

- Children who are taught that they should look smart instead of loving learning tend to develop a fixed mindset.
- They become more concerned with how they are being judged and fear that they might not live up to expectations.

Growth Mindsets

- Children who are taught to explore, embrace new experiences, and enjoy challenges are more likely to develop a growth mindset.
- Rather than seeing mistakes as setbacks, they are willing to try new things and make errors all in the name of learning and achieving their potential.

Fixed mindsets	Growth mindsets
Limited Beliefs	Growth
Judgment - Feeling judged	Learn to trust yourself
Time – The feeling of not enough time	Practice perseverance and patience
Failure – Worried about failing	Become resilient and take it as an opportunity
Opinionated – Scared to voice your opinion	Believe you have something important to say, have confidence in yourself

Loneliness	Opportunity to be independent and choose your crowd that align with your future self

Adjusting your mindset is key to hope because you can find solutions to overcome problems with a different perspective. It is all about your perspective and how you see the world. It is not about being positive all the time but it is about making the best out of each situation and being hopeful. The definition of hopeful is confident, optimistic and encouraging. Growth mindsets can characterise hopefulness. Once you have hope for your future, it is easier to create a new one.

Most of the time the thing that is holding you back is lack of self-confidence. So you need to analyse where this thought pattern is coming from and change the story. Maybe you have low confidence because you feel like you never fit into the social conditioning group, maybe it is from a past trauma or simply because you never felt unconditional love (yes, this is deep). Whatever the reason, you have the option to recondition your mind and believe a different narrative.

CHANGE YOUR INNER STORY

We often have a story that we tell ourselves daily, it is the way we perceive our life. We often play the victim in our own lives and this is what holds us back from achieving or expanding. We think our life circumstances and situations are not in our control, that life is happening to us rather than for us. Some people experience different levels of this than others (I am not talking about genuine victims of abuse here), depending on the type of environment they have been brought up in and how their neuron pathways have been formed. However, we all experience some form of victim mentality though social conditioning, where we have been indoctrinated to feel victimised. When we adopt this mentality, we lose all our power and forget our own strengths in our authenticity. Culture often wants us to feel less than we are so we consume more, creating the cycle of consuming to feel whole and empowered (buy the fast car, sexy dress etc). We are sold the victim mentality through culture so we stay small.

"Live life as if everything is rigged in your favour" – Edith Wharton

Charles R Snyder, an American psychologist (1944-2006) wrote a book called Positive Psychology and several books on the theory of hope, now remembered as a pioneer of the positive psychology movement. Snyder's, Hope Theory takes into consideration cognitive and affective elements. Suggesting that hope leads to motivation, and that goals, paths and freedom of choice help generate hope.

The Hope Theory distinguishes two main ways of thinking that formulate a good basis for setting achievable goals and creating hope. These two ways of thinking are called Pathway Thinking and Agency Thinking. Pathway Thinking is based on the idea of cognitive ability to produce a pathway to reach a goal. Whereas, Agency Thinking is based on the amount of confidence and intention that we have on reaching the goal. Snyder theory suggests that we have the ability to dissolve our victim mentality by using hope as a method and change our inner story by setting achievable goals.

That being said we all have the ability to change our inner story, one of the major breakthrough in my life was looking at hindsight and realising that everything I had experienced in life (the good, bad and ugly), had led to me where I am now. Without these experiences, I wouldn't have the knowledge and confidence within myself to speak my truth and make an impact, I wouldn't have the courage to step-up and live my life on my terms, which ultimately makes me feel more fulfilled (coming from a place of purpose). Occasionally, I used to adopt the victim mentality and think things were out of my control but once I changed my inner story, I realised I could deal with whatever life throws at me (that I am safe either way). Look at your life as if you are the narrator, that you are not reading a story but creating one.

For example:

Lake of confidence – What is holding you back?	Story – Why you believe this?	Change – take action steps to create a new story
Example – No one will listen to what you have to say, you feel unheard, you believe you are not interesting enough to speak your truth.	You feel this way because you felt unloved when you were young, maybe feeling of neglect, condemnation or opposing parents.	Believe you have something important worth saying, trust yourself. Start speaking to those that understand you and hold the same values as you so they can relate to your message.

When you have a future full of hope then you will be ambitious. You will find it easier to create the life or business that your desire. Just by making a few changes to your thought process over time, will make big difference (I say over time because transforming your mindset takes dedication). With a growth mindset you will be able to adapt to change and not feel overwhelmed.

COMMUNITY

Once you have the confidence to grow your own grass and hopeful future then it is time to find your tribe. Likeminded people that can support your growth.

Have you ever noticed how digital nomads gather together? Even though they are working remotely and independently, they work from co-working spaces; the 'co' stands for company. It is in our human behaviour to seek those that understand us and share the same values, this is down to survival instinct. It is in our DNA to be around people with the same habitation, simply because more means stronger.

This is nothing new, throughout history, people have gathered for support and strength. From tribal gatherings to the board room. Your tribe reflects your vibe, you attract the kind of people you need in your life at the right time. It is a part of the universal pull, the people that you surround yourself with are fundamental to your growth. So be sure to surround yourself with those that inspire you and have your best interest at heart. Being in a group of people that inspire you can fill you with confidence and motivate you to live your best life, whether that is starting a new hobby, project or business.

Be in an environment where you can thrive. Being in a place where you feel supported and can be yourself is necessary for your health, wellbeing and ability to achieve your potential. If you're in the right environment you will feel confident, more productive and able to flourish.

Have you ever felt like your environment is hindering your progress? Or not making you feel of value or simply going against your morals? Have you felt the difference depending on where you are and who you are with? Make sure those around you are supporting you! If something is not nourishing you, then make the change! Seek those that help your thrive!

SOLAR PLEXUS CHAKRA

The Solar Plexus Chakra, otherwise known as the Manipura is the third Chakra, located above the navel (as we work our way up the body). It is home to our personal power, willpower, self-esteem, self-discipline, responsibility and self-respect; representing the perception of oneself and balancing the ego. When balanced it helps face challenges in life and become motivated to meet that goal you set for yourself. Based around the core area, it is about your inner strength and ability succeed. With strong faith in one's ability and hope, you will be able to achieve anything you set your mind to. This Chakra follows on from the Sacral Chakra, once the sense of self is developed then you can work on your motivation and willpower. Helping you to be more proactive, than reactive or inactive. For example, when this chakra not balanced and there is an excess of energy in this area, then we will react to life circumstances and feel stressed. If the energy is blocked then we will be inactive, passive, allowing life to go by without acting. However, when the chakra is balanced, we will be able to move forward in life with confidence and power, making conscious decisions and being able to act on them.

The third Chakra is physically associated with the central metabolic system, digestive system; including the stomach, liver, intestines and pancreas. These areas of the body control the chemical substance, insulin in our body, which regulates the amount of sugar in our blood. Therefore, the more insulin we have, the more energy we have. However, these too can be overactive or underactive. Where we can have too much energy and feel anxious or too little and feel fatigue. The idea is to get a healthy balance, so we are motivated to perform our daily tasks and duties, but not too much where we will get burnt-out.

What does this look like:

Overactive	Underactive
Aggressive	Weak willpower
Critical of one's self and others	Lack of self esteem
Controlling	Lake of self-control
Fear of rejection	Unreliable
Judgmental	No motivation
	Lake of commitment

To balance this Chakra, it is good to work on self-discipline, by performing tasks and goals for yourself that you know you can meet, this will allow space to set bigger macro goals. Once you generate self-discipline, you know that you can rely on yourself, therefore becoming more reliable for others. This will spring you forward, knowing you can achieve goals, will make you feel more motivated to set new ones. The more you do this, the more you will create stronger neuro pathways in your brain and it will become second nature to you.

Knowing that you can change your behaviour and thought process by using neuro plasticity, will help you develop and create new neuro pathways in your brain that align with what you want to do or achieve.

EXERCISE 3: STRENGHTENING YOUR GROWTH MINDSET

As we have discovered, we can change our mindset through neuro plasticity, this means we can create change. Change of mindset and environment. Which can be achieved by being in the right environment, one that strengthens your mission and builds your confidence.

Think about what you want to achieve or do, then question what is holding you back from doing it? Is it your mindset, your inner story or your environment? Make note of who is around you, in your environment. Are they hindering your progress or are they supporting you?

Environment	The relationship you have with the person in that environment	Are they supporting your Growth Mindset?

Now let's focus on what you want to achieve and having the willpower and self-determination to bring it to life and make it happen. It might seem miles away from where you are now (that is okay) but it is a start. Think about your lifestyle, how can you take action steps forward, through the daily choices that you make and actions you take (for example, if being fit and healthy is a goal but all your friends party excessively and you sit at home eating pizza every day, these actions aren't going to help you get where you want to be. So change the story).

Make a list of your small micro goals and big macro goals. The micro goals are things you want to achieve and seem reachable. Things that you already know that you are capable of achieving. The macro goals are bigger goals that might take some time and development to get there. If you identify your bigger goals then you can find a way to make them happen. Start planning ahead, do what you can in the now (present) for your future. We all have to start somewhere.

Small Micro Goals	Bigger Macro Goals	How are you going to take steps to achieve them?

CHAPTER FOUR:

BLOOMING
HEART

Now you are more aware of your thought patterns, what you want to achieve and have a greater willpower to creative a new narrative for yourself, it is time to be creative and innovative, to bring your idea to life.

Being in the right environment can allow creative thinking to flow. What does that mean? It means, as we discover new things our brain is activated. Therefore, creativity and innovation come more naturally to us. This means expanding, exploring, and learning – keeping the brain active. For example – we cannot bloom in an environment that is distracting us, making us feel inadequate. We need to be in the right space to be in the right mind frame for creativity.

The trick is to always keep your brain activated. Through neuroscience we discover the connection between our brain and how we feel. How do we activate the brain to be innovative?

Creativity, innovation and manifestation have the same fundamental meaning. They are all bringing something to life. This is why the right side of the brain is considered to be more feminine because women are natural creators (life givers). This is relating back to Chapter two, but of course, both men and women can be equally creative.

| Idea | ➡ | Create | ➡ | Business | ➡ | Enterprise |

Whether, you have a project, product, invention, or design. It all started from an idea, a seed planted in your mind – then it is created into a tangible, physical form and potentially into a sustainable, thriving business.
Neuroscientist, Richard. J. Davidson said that "A wandering mind is an unhappy mind". This means that we often find ourselves 'wandering' when we are bored, not focused or doing a mundane task. Therefore, we need to have an interest in something to be happy – when we are interested in something we are focused. For example – Have you ever read one or two chapters of a book and had no idea what you have just read? Have you ever driven somewhere and when you arrive have no memory of the journey? This is because our

mind goes into autopilot with a lot of activities we do. We repeat actions without engaging in them or activating our mind. In order to focus, we need to create new neuro pathways that activate our mind, to keep it alive.

Four ways to create new neuro pathways

UNHAPPY	HAPPY
Distractibility	Awareness
Loneliness	Connections
Negative Self Talk	Insight, change the narrative
Loss of Purpose	Purpose

The opposite to distractibility is awareness (or awakening). When our brain is activated, we become aware. This can be through our senses (smell, touch, sight and hearing), intellectual stimulation or physical activities. By making a change in our habits and actions then we can create new neuro pathways in our brain. Which can lead to creativity or innovation.

By creating a sense of purpose for yourself, you will create happy hormones in your brain so you will feel more fulfilled. This doesn't have to be a grand gesture, it can also mean finding joy in the small things in life. Giving the little things we do meaning or a sense of value. But it also can mean starting a new business venture, creating a product or service that aligns with your truth and creates a sense of purpose for yourself or for others.

PURPOSE

Have you ever wondered what your purpose in life is, what you are meant to be doing on this earth? This is your dharma, meaning your soul purpose, way of living and the nature of reality regarded as a universal truth. In Buddhism, dharma means "cosmic law and order", as applied to the teachings of Buddha and can be applied to mental constructs or what is recognised by the mind. In Buddhist philosophy dharma is also the term for "phenomena".

Dharma: refers to one's duty in this life, dharma is your purpose that you set out to do in life. It is the end goal, whereas karma is what you do to get to the end goal. The idea is mentioned in many different philosophical writings and used in different religions. However, it is more than living the 'right' way, it is about living your truth.

How can this be applied in modern day life? Fundamentally it means loving what you do or feeling fulfilled, this can be translated into passion, drive, intention, whatever feels good for the soul and makes us feel alive. Dharma is a concept that can be used in modern day life so we can live a life of fulfilment and purpose, living as our higher self. But to be able to do this we need to start analysing our thoughts and actions, why we think the way we do. How have we been conditioned to live by society, culture, religion to gain social acceptance and status. Only way in which we can find true purpose is if we start to trust and listen to ourselves, rather then what society has told us. Cutting out the outside noise can create a clear vision and give clarity.

The number one key to purpose or dharma is acting with consciousness so in order to achieve this we need to start critical thinking, thinking for ourselves rather then what we 'should' do (mentioned in chapter one). This clears the path, creates clarity for us to focus on what we want to do, that brings us fulfilment.

If we have a sense of purpose at work or know we are making a positive impact on another person, community, or the world, then it provokes the feeling that we matter, that our actions matter. Why? Because our brain releases one of the four happy chemicals when we accomplish something. These chemicals are dopamine, serotonin, oxytocin and endorphins. It is natural that we want them turned on all the time so we constantly feel happy, however these chemicals are only produced as a reward (not to be turned on all the time). They are designed to encourage and promote our survival. They are released when we see something we want or want to do, like a goal (work target, admired person or reaching a location). They are more stimulated the closer we get to it, when we see the end in sight, we release more dopamine in the brain. However, when we reach the goal then it stops because it is no longer needed, the happy chemicals are no longer produced because we have what we want. The more we practice a sport, the better we get at it because our brain is creating new neuron pathways every time we play, the stronger the pathways, the better we become at the sport (this can be the same for work). Once a neuro pathway is formed, it becomes easier to reach the goal and produce happy chemicals. Therefore, the more often we do something that makes us feel fulfilled, the more rewarded we will feel. It is a constant and evolving process, mainly built on our survival (if we think we need something to live or do something).

"You don't find happiness, you create it"- Katarina Blom

The best way to find your purpose is to create, this is not something you can find because it is not external. If we can create value in what we do then we can create the sense of purpose in our life. By making something valuable then we add meaning and purpose to it, likewise with actions, if our actions are giving a sense of value then it gives purpose to what we are doing. When we create value around a subject then our brain recognises this as a survival technique and acts in the same way, creating happy chemicals.

So how do we create value? The Value Theory looks at this concept and describes the idea of value as good. What we perceive to be good, what feels good for your soul. The only way we can truly know this is by following our intuition (look at chapters two and three). However, there is a fine line between distinguishing what makes us feel good and what we have been told is good. This is why it is so important to question your reality and the reasons you feel certain ways about things. Once you know what feels genuinely good for your soul then it is easier to act with value and therefore purpose.

| What we percieve to be good | Added value | Purpose | Fulfillment |

Some people find purpose in helping others, seeing other people happy makes them feel fulfilled, which would be a service type of business (consulting agency, customer service or yoga teaching for example). Other like creating or solving problems which could mean creating a new product or system. Whatever, brings you the most fulfilment will make you feel like you are acting with purpose.

CREATIVITY

To be innovative, you have to tap into your creative mind (as mentioned in chapter two) but in order to make a successful business you need purpose and strategy behind the creativity, this will give you drive to move forward.

When I was studying for my MA (masters) in Innovation and Entrepreneurship, almost everyone on the course already had their own business. We were already had the idea but wanted to execute it into successful business. To be able to take our products/service to market while targeting the right customers. So, what did we do? 1) Business Model Canvas 2) USP 3) SWOT 4) Cash Flow 5) Bowmans Clock. However the real breakthrough happened when we each discovered a solution to a problem or need. If you can solve a problem with your product or service, it is highly likely that people will want or need it.

Michael Kirton (1976-2003) once suggested that, if you can make a product or a service that solves a problem then this is creativity. Being able to solve a problem means you have to think of a new way of doing something. Kirton created the Adaptation-Innovation Theory. The theory suggests that there are two types of people that solve problems, the Adaptation people and the Innovative people. While the Adaptation people solve problems by using what resources are given, the Innovative people solve a problem by looking beyond what resources are in front of them. The Adapters like to make something 'better' and the Innovators like to do something 'different'. This suggests that the Adaptors thinks inside the box, however the Innovators thinks outside of the box.

"Adapters prefer to do well within the given paradigm, Innovators would rather do differently, thereby striving to transcend the existing paradigm" – Kirton

Which one do you think you are? There is no right or wrong answer, however it is important to acknowledge which way you work. This will give you more clarity and be able to create solutions more effectively. This is help you understand your thought process. Knowing that you have the ability to be creative no matter which category applies to you.

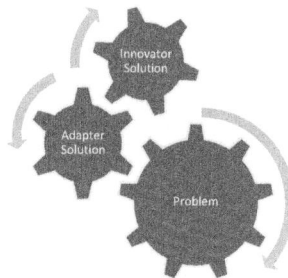

HEART CHAKRA

The heart chakra is all about your passion and purpose. It is also known as Anahata which translates to "unhurt." This chakra is where your love, compassion, and kindness are empowered. We all associate the heart chakra with love and that is exactly what it is, but it includes every area of your life, not just in a romantic sense. It can mean being in love with what you do. Having a job or business that brings you a sense of fulfilment and purpose. It is about being truly happy in the role you are in.

This Chakra is located in the heart centre and is related to the upper body. It effects our lungs, heart, arms, hands, thymus glands procedures lymphocytes and immune system. When we are in balance these areas work healthily and effectively. When out of balance, there maybe poor blood circulation, high blood pressure, pain in the upper back and shoulders and stiff joints.

Symptoms look like:

Overactive	Underactive
Jealousy	Difficulty trusting
Lack of independence	Feeling rejected or lonely
Over give or no boundaries	Under give or no compassion

When this chakra is balanced, we both have compassion for others, one's self and the work that we do. However, if the chakra is out of balance it may mean that you are overcompensating for others or over working, which can make you feel de-valued. The aim is to put value and purpose into what you do. Literally, putting your heart into what you do, in every aspect of your life (love for one's self, other and leading from a place of love). This then in turn will generate the feeling of fulfilment and joy.

EXERCISE 4: CREATING A SENSE OF PURPOSE

As we know solving a problem or reaching a goal creates happy chemicals in our brain, giving us a sense of purpose. If we want to love what we do then we need to find a solution for a problem in the marketplace or for our customers. What are your customer needs? Are you able to create a product or service that fulfils these needs? Once you know this, it will become your purpose, it will be your mission statement.

So, I propose that you create a mission statement for yourself, something that you intent to offer the world as your purpose, what can you provide?

My mission statement is:	....

CHAPTER FIVE:

COMMUNICATION
THROAT

How we send and receive information is vital for efficient communication. It is important to be conscientious on how you are sending information to another person so they can receive it effectively. Speak your truth, come from a place of authenticity and others will be able to relate to you. Be conscientious about what language you use, not just for others but also yourself because what we say, sends receptive signals to the brain where we form our opinions and understanding.

There are many neuros in the brain constantly sending information between pathways. Myelin coats the axon nerve fibres, supporting efficient communication between the neuros in the brain, it is insulation for the neuro pathways (myelination is the process of building this). The more two people communicate, the more likely they are to form a connection; just like the brain, the neuro pathways become more reinforced and able to send and receive messages from one neuro to another more effectively. So by building better communication strategies, we form deeper connections which allows more understanding and clarity. The more often we do this, the more our neuro pathways are stronger and being able to receive messages becomes easier.

Communication in the brain is split up into two areas; the way we receive information is in one area, called Wernickes area (named after Brian Wernicke), this is located in area 22 of the brain. The way we express ourselves is in another area of the brain, called Brocas area (named after Paul Broca), this is located in area 44 and 45 of the brain. So we have two area of the brain, one for receiving information and ones from sending information. Both of these need to be performing well in order to have effective communication and build connections. As communication is not only about speaking, it is equally about listening.

SPEAKER	LISTENER
Left Front Lobule (44 & 45)	Temporal Lobule (22)
Expressive	Receptive
Speech Production	Language Comprehension

Language Comprehension	Sensory
Speech Related Gestures	
Motor	

The speaker and the listener areas in the brain have different functions and are in different areas. In order for our communication to be at the highest level of efficiency, these need to be working equally well, to send and receive messages. The Inferior Parietal Lobule helps the neuro pathways (our internal system) to run smoothly. Also known as Geschwind's territory after Norman Geschwind, an American neurologist, who in the early 1960s foresaw its importance. It connects both areas together and helps interpret sensory information.

COMMUNICATION SYSTEMS

To communicate effectively we need to create a system, like the function of the Inferior parietal lobule in our brain, that helps transfer information between areas. The reason there is often a breakdown in communication is because these connections have not been made and we don't understand one another. In order to form connections, we need to create communication strategies that work for both individuals. It has been proven that the more transparent we are, the more clarity is formed. Just like eye contact.

Michael Platt, a neuroscientist has mentioned the importance of forming social connections. As we are social creatures and perform better when we are working together. The role of a leader is to make this happen, to connect to the people they manage and create an environment where they can work together efficiently. Research shows that eye contact plays a major part in communication. If we look into someone eyes, we form a bond, have better chemistry and start to mirror each other, therefore creating synchronicity and better communication.

So, the more transparent, the better at expressing information and the more open minded we are, the better we will be at receiving information.

In today's society we are constantly being fed information, the information we receive by advertising and marketing companies has been made to activate our sensory system. Therefore, creating customer engagement. This used to be done in face to face sales, creating the human connection. Now, with the increase in online activity, this is being done by collecting data about each individual and using to make them feel like they have a bond with the product or service. It is important to note that there are marketing systems created to get our attention, either by collecting data about what individual likes and dislikes or posting images that stimulate their brain sensors. As we are doing more and more things online, more and more information is being collected about us and the used to grab our attention and sell products. Neuroscience is used a lot in marketing and sales, advertising companies have a whole strategy and system in place to collect data about each customer and then use this data to connect with them. There is much evidence that suggests that our natural human connection is being lost (face to face) and a digital connection is being programmed. It is almost like we are being read, however we cannot see the receiver. Whereas, in face to face connection it is a two-way connection of receiving and giving information. You can tell how the other person reacts to the information you give them by their facial expressions, you can also tell if someone is being authentic by their facial expressions (you are aware if they are being truthful). This forms interpersonal connection. However, if there is a disconnection between the two parties, like the digital age, we cannot tell how the other person is receiving the information and who is giving us the information. Our neuro connection system is working, we are receiving information, however it is algorithm based.

To be a conscious leader or thinker then we need to be aware of such systems. And create a system that is authentic and works ethically to connect to our customers or team. Being transparent helps customers or team members identify with the service or product message, and is a more ethical way of doing business. If you are a conscientious thinker, leader or brand, then why not use it to your advantage and tell your customers why you are conscientious. However, the most important thing is being authentic, this helps build solid relations and trust. It will also help you to feel more fulfilled and positive for expressing yourself in an authentic way (speaking your truth). For when we express ourselves in an authentic way we are being honest, to one's self and others. And when we are honest, we are more open to both giving and receiving, in speaking and listening.

If you are going to be a manager, leader or entrepreneur then it is your responsibility to connect with your team and customers. Therefore, it is important to be aware of business to customer relations. There are two sales business models, business-to-business (B2B) and business-to-consumer (B2C). The business to consumer model focuses on selling directly to the customer which is the end user. The business to business sells to another business, this is like wholesales orders or recruitment agencies, there is a middleman included so you are not selling to the end user. Both models have wide range of performing in business and both have proven to perform well. In order for these models to run effectively, there needs to be a robust communication system in place. So information is passed along effectively. The B2B communication takes on a more business lead approach to communication, this is more formal. However, the B2C approach should be more fluid depending on the individual, building more of a interpersonal connection with the customers. This is where it gets interesting, knowing your market and being able to be authentic and transparent in that market will help you form deeper connections with your customers and get re-occurring sales by building on customer loyalty. So basically the more you walk and talk in your authentic self, this will build transparency and clarity, therefore leading to customer connections.

THROAT CHAKRA

The fifth chakra is called Vasudha which translates to "very pure" or the Throat charka as it is located in the throat area. This is about speaking your truth, coming from a place of pure intention and being able to express and articulate yourself well. This has a strong reference to communication, communicating clearly, confidently, and honestly. Being able to express your needs and vision amongst others so in turn they can understand and connect with you.

Buddha once said, "before you say anything, ask yourself, is it true? Is it necessary? And is it kind?

It is very closely connected to the third chakra, where we hold our willpower and confidence. Being able to express one's self truly, means that we must have the confidence to do so, it takes courage and bravery. If this area is under active then it means there is still work to be done in the third chakra (chapter three). Not having confidence or self-discipline can hinder you to speak your truth with conviction.

To balance the throat chakra, pay attention to your neck, bring movement into this area and do some breath work. A great exercise is doing head rolls, as you roll your head forwards take an inhale and as you roll your head back take the exhale. You can also try Lions Breath, this is intended to both empower you and give you confidence to speak your truth. Simply, stick your tongue out and take a deep exhale. It is best to do this in the mirror to make the connection and identify with yourself.

EXERCISE 5: SPEAKING YOUR TRUTH

As discussed in this chapter, when we speak our truth we form authentic connections with those around us. Two big components of speaking your truth is Transparency and Truth. By speaking from a place of authenticity in a transparent way, this will help build connection by forming stronger neuropathways between two people. This being said, it is highly important to articulate yourself in a way that the receiver will understand. A great way to do this is to explain the why. Then when you are receiving information, recognise what the other person is saying and ask yourself why they are saying it.

This can be used for expressing your feelings, suggesting an idea or setting a task.

What you want to communicate	Why do you want to communicate this, your reasoning

Notes:

CHAPTER SIX:

THE STORM
THIRD EYE

Criticism is the practice of judging the merits and faults of something

We all have faced a storm at some part in our lives, that period in time where everything feels heavy, like a whirlwind has hit you. In business, it is likely that you will experience many set-backs like this, and when we do, we often feel like giving up. We believe it is not possible to do and self-doubt creeps in. However, these set-backs are just challenges and if we start to see them objectively, then they can become a challenge that we can overcome (and dare I say it, learn from). These challenges can be changed into opportunities; Imagine a bow and arrow, the arrow has to be pulled back before it can swing forwards.

The biggest critic in our lives, is one's self. There are two main critics, internally and externally. While we cannot control the external, how other people act, we can control our reactions. From doing the inner work (healing and mindfulness), we can begin to see the world from a new perspective, therefore being able to act with wisdom and compassion, rather than reacting. This means that when we are faced with external criticism, we are not affected as we take an objective approach and choose how we act. We do not perceive it personally or take it as constructive criticism.

"Imagine if you had a friend who constantly pointed out everything that was wrong with you and your life. You'd probably want to get rid of them right away" - Olivia Remes

THE INNER CRITIC

We have all experienced those people that are condescending and critical, and we often don't want to be around them. But often we do this to ourselves. We criticise ourselves for not achieving enough, for not making the salary bonus, for not being attractive and so on. We often feel that we are not reaching our goals or that others are achieving more. This is simply because we have been brought up into a word that thrives on self-doubt and comparison. We form these ideals early on in childhood, either through caregivers, religion, social or culture conditioning. This is where we form cognitive behaviour patterns.

Cognition is "the mental action or process of acquiring knowledge and understanding through thought, experience, and the senses.

It is important to embrace the idea that there is no positive or negative mindset because as humans we get both thoughts daily. It is not possible to eliminate all negative thoughts from our mind, however we can learn to accept and choose again. When something triggers us into a negative mind frame, we can take a step back to view and gain a new perspective or focus. It's important to remember that thoughts are not facts! So if you get negative thoughts, acknowledge it for what it is, a simple thought, and it can be changed by shifting our   focus.

We all have come from different backgrounds and had different experiences, these experiences shape the way we feel and act. Our minds are programmed at a young age and these can shape our thought processes. The way we think about ourselves, others and situations. This is called cognitive behaviour.

90% of our happiness is to do with how we see the world. Is your **"physical environment supporting our mental health"?** And what can we do to change it. Sometimes we need to change our physical environment and sometimes we need to change our perspective. Shifting your cognitive behaviour in a more productive way will produce more Dopamine (the happy hormone), resulting in reducing blood pressure, improving the immune system and becoming more productive.

How you can overcome your inner critic and recondition your behaviour?

One way we can change our cognitive behaviour is to act in the present moment (rather than worrying about the past or future), this creates awareness and we become less reactional and more rational. Another way is to do things that make you feel good and reflect your values, this releases neurotransmitters such as endorphins. Physical activity also stimulates the release of dopamine, norepinephrine, and serotonin. These brain chemicals play an important part in regulating your mood.
By releasing these positive hormones we can then gain a new perspective; this therefore builds self-confidence within, rather than looking for outward pleasures or conformations. Knowing ourselves and being present in the moment, stops us from worrying about the past or

future. It allows us to take in what is happening in the now, evaluate and choose where we want to focus.

Reconditioning steps:

1) Identifying the feeling, acknowledging when you're feeling anxious and why.
2) Accepting the feeling led us to understand why we feel a certain way. This often takes courage because once we acknowledge what we don't like, we have to change it or live in self-denial which will tear your soul apart.
3) Choosing again, choose to be in control of your emotions instead of being reactive. Almost everything in life is uncertain, so unless we restructure our minds we will always be in a state of anxiety. The key is to program our minds with a feeling of hope, faith and choice. So even if we find ourselves in a uncomfortable situation, we know that we have the choice to leave the situation and that it will not last forever. Some might say, it happened for the greater good.

The important to remember that is we have the ability to change, as mentioned previously, we can create new neuro pathways in our mind though Neuro plasticity. So we can change our cognitive behaviour.

THE EXTERNAL CRITIC

Once you have mastered the internal critic, it is a lot easier to handle external criticism. There are two types of external criticism that we are often faced with, other human behaviour and our external environment (feeling that anything around us is going wrong).

1. Environment

Sometimes it is pure FACT, life can be shit! I am a dreamer but also a realist and sometimes we can be faced with challenges that seem too big to overcome or get through. I remember being made redundant form my job, relationship falling apart and having to move out of my house all at the same time. These things do have a habit of hitting you all at once. And it might seem overwhelming (to say the least)! The only way to really get thought it is to know that you are safe no matter what happens. I used to get myself into a rabbit hole of thought trails, of thinking the worst-case scenario. If something was challenging me, I would just feel the earth under my feet crumble and not feel safe. This is why so many people suffer from stress and anxiety because fundamentally they don't feel safe. Our nervous system gets turned on autopilot and we move into fight or flight mode. So it is essential that we remember that we are safe in difficult situations or environments.

Understanding the nervous system

We have two nervous systems, the parasympathetic and the sympathetic. The parasympathetic nervous system moderates organs such as glands when in rest and digest mode, however the sympathetic nerve system moderates our actions and bodily function response when in threat. It gets activated in times of fear so we can maintain homeostasis self-regulation. The sympathetic nervous system goes all the way down the spinal cord. When we feel under threat, this gets activated and has an impact our body and response.

The nervous system is complex, however the key here is to establish that you are safe, no matter what environment you are in so you can retain a sense of homeostasis. This means your body is balanced between the two nervous systems and then you can make conscientious choices and responses.

Sympathetic Nerve System	Parasympathetic Nerve System
Controls bodies response while in threat	Controls bodies response while in rest
Fight or Flight Mode	Rest or Digest Mode
Heart rate increase	Heart rate decreases
Increase blood flow to muscles	Decrease blood flow to muscles
Increase in mobility & digestion	Decrease in mobility and digestion
Airways constrict (Bronchial)	Airways dilate (Bronchial)

2. Human Behaviour

When someone offends you, criticises you personally or your work, remember that this is a reflection on their behaviour, do not take it personally. I know this is easier said than done. However, the more you practice the below OBJECTIVE METHOD the easier it will become. If someone is underestimating you or being critical of the new path you have taken of stepping away from the mainstream system, remember that you are doing something that has never been done before so some people might not understand. You don't have to justify your actions or decisions to others, especially if they are not willing to listen or understand.

If you have chosen the path of the Black Sheep, conscientious thinker, innovator. You are basically choosing a path that is not the norm, stepping away from society and cultural conditioning to make your own life rules. You are escaping the culture scape. So, you will be on the side of the minority. Unfortunately, there are fewer free thinkers than followers, so you have to be prepared for some people not to understand you. There might even be people that are envious of you for having the courage and motivation to make the change, follow your own path instead of the system. If this occurs, remember chapter two.

Start seeing criticism as judgment from the creator (the person where the judgment comes from), not the receiver. It is the view of the person judging, it is simply and only their opinion. It is simply a thought, not reality. The reason someone judges another is because they are not content within and therefore look externally to feel satisfaction. If they don't get it from others they will criticise. So learn to let go of judgment – I have experienced this myself, I was judged by a family member for not having the same views as them and taking a different outlook on life. The weight of their judgment was heavy, It took time for me to recognise this is coming from them and not a reflection on myself. That I need to be free from this judgment in order to proceed on my journey.

There is no quick fix, sometimes you have to work through the criticism and examine your own shadows to understand why it is affecting you. This could be because you don't trust your own decisions because your caregivers didn't show they trusted you to do so. It could be because you don't know your own worth after feeling betrayed in the past or felt like you had to fight for attention growing up. Or it could be that you need to set firmer boundaries with people, you let people walk all over you because you are a people pleaser, always felt like you had to please your caregivers to receive love and affection. We all have shadow work that we need to do, to release the shadows that hold us back from living the life we want.

Look at the OBJECTIVE METHOD below to examine how you can let go of criticism, judgment and your shadow. To start taking action steps, so you are more in control of your feelings, thoughts and actions.

The two best ways to react to criticism is:

1) Don't react – take a step back from the situation or person

2) Act with love – start to see others less like an enemy, trying to hurt you and more like someone that has their own shadow work to deal with. Treat them with love and compassion, not in a condescending way (condescending is the opposite as it is putting another person down so you feel better). Instead,

say you might not agree but understand where they are coming from.

Don't play the victim – When you play the victim, you give all your power away. The world wants us all to feel like a victim, so we feel lost, weak and look externally for validation. The truth is, no one is coming to save you so get up and be your own saviour, look internally and trust yourself. Do what you need to do, to take control over your feelings and thoughts, you are capable of changing your neuro network (chapter three).

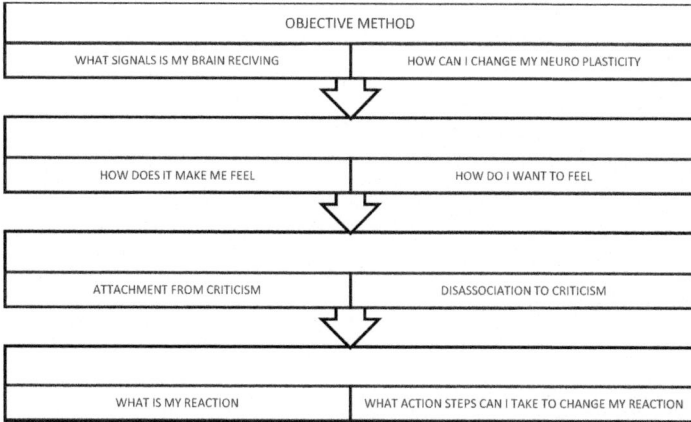

OBJECTIVE METHOD	
WHAT SIGNALS IS MY BRAIN RECIVING	HOW CAN I CHANGE MY NEURO PLASTICITY

HOW DOES IT MAKE ME FEEL	HOW DO I WANT TO FEEL

ATTACHMENT FROM CRITICISM	DISASSOCIATION TO CRITICISM

WHAT IS MY REACTION	WHAT ACTION STEPS CAN I TAKE TO CHANGE MY REACTION

CHALLENGE OR OPPORTUNITY

With an objective outlook, we can start to see challenges as opportunities. When something is not working then it forces us to re-evaluate it. This is where some of the best ideas and projects come from. Start by asking yourself how can I make it better, what can I do or implement? Maybe it is giving you an opportunity to be innovative or adaptable, remember solving a problem is a part of creativity.

For example, Disney theme parks were one of the most innovative ideas of the 20th century, everyone wanted to go until it got almost too busy and the queues got too big. People started to get frustrated and there were new competitors in the market place (and sales started to fall). Did Walt give up? NO! Him and his team examined what was going on in the market at large and the customer needs, to come up with a new idea, having electronic wrist bands that were sent to the consumer by post (leaving out the queues).

Below is a basic SWOT analysis diagram, for every weakness there is a strength and for every threat there is an opportunity. When we take an objective view of every threat and weakness, we will be able to find the strength and opportunity. By taking an objective approach, we gain a bigger overview which is impartial. Being able to examine a threat or weakness from a neutral position, allows space for a new perspective.

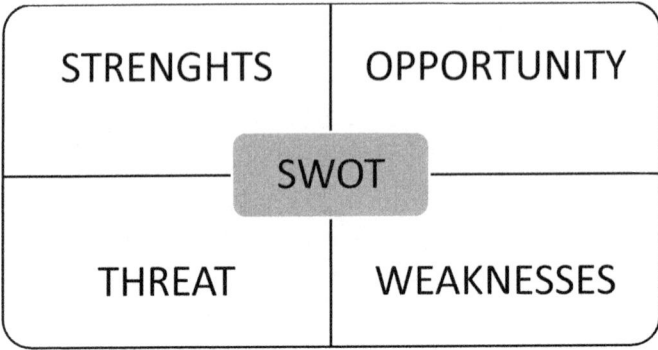

COMPARTMENTALISATION

Compartmentalisation helps us cope with the feeling of being overwhelmed, especially if you are an entrepreneur juggling many different tasks and jobs within their business. We only have a certain number of hours in the day and sometimes it may feel like we are doing several full-time jobs. We can feel overwhelmed when we have many things that demand our attention and time. Have you ever felt this? Compartmentalisation enables you to examine each area and divide them into sections and categories. This makes each area smaller and more manageable. Being able to work through them one step at a time. Not only does this allow you to feel less overwhelmed it can also create a system where you tackle each thing at a time. You might have some areas of your life or business that are performing really well and you might have other areas that need some work.

This is where it is good to activate the left side of your brain, the planning, strategy and organisation. Once we have a plan in place, then things will run a lot smoother and we will be able to tackle each issue (weakness or threat). By building a compartmentalisation strategy, we will have a logical view (not emotional) of the scenario. Being able to analyse what needs to be done and the time frame. For example, in my business we use a pivot table (but you can use another resource) to track the supply chain. You can also use this strategy when expanding your team, by acknowledging what you have time for and what jobs you need to outsource or assign to another person. By activating the left side of the brain, we can find composure.

Below is an example of how you can categorise aspects of your business (this can be used in different areas of your life too), just by acknowledging what you are capable of. Once you know how much time you want to designate to each areas in your life then you can outsource the other areas, to make it more manageable. Ultimately it would be more beneficial if you spend time on the aspect that aligns with your authenticity. The key here is to spend time on the thing that you feel passionate about or the skill you attain.

If you can't afford to outsource areas then it is extremely important to compartmentalise your mindset, designating time to each specific area.

MARKETING

CUSTOMER RELATIONS

DESIGNATE OUTSOURCE

PRODUCTION

YOU

OPERATIONS

DESIGNING

YOU

MANAGEMENT

THIRD EYE CHAKRA

This chakra is the sixth in the sequence, it is represented as the third eye (on your forehead in between each eye) which means vision. Your vision of the world and your chosen path. Bringing awareness and clarity into what you do by knowing your so-called calling, purpose or dharma (what ever you prefer to call it). If this Chakra is balanced, you will have insight into your mission and a strong sense of self awareness. By knowing who you are, will help you take an objective outlook on any problems you may face because you will see beyond them, and have a wider perspective.

It is linked to the Pituitary and Pineal glands, the Hypothalamus Pituitary nerve plexus which governs the autonomic nervous system and the pituitary in the endocrine system. The Pituitary gland is a master glade that produces hormones to control your growth and bodily development. Whilst the Pineal gland controls your sleeping and waking patterns. Paying attention to the upper body, around your head and brain region. These glands are responsible for making sure you have enough sleep to function well in everyday life with a clear head.

Symptoms may appear as:

Overactive	Underactive
Lack of good judgment	Unable to self-reflect
Minimum observation	Lack of faith in your purpose

Not connected to reality or truth	Stubborn or close-minded
Over self-righteous and extroverted	Introverted

When this chakra is out of balance then we can feel overwhelmed, however when the chakra is balanced we have the ability to have deep insight and clarity. This is where the mind and body connect, bringing into force both the left and right side of the brain, for intellect and intuition. A lot of transformation happens in this Chakra, if it is balanced then we have the ability to alchemise and transcend situation with our perspective. By Consciously elevating and transmuting situations using our intellect and intuition.

EXERCISE 6: LEARN HOW TO ALCHEMISE

If we have the ability to turn a weakness into a strength and a threat into an opportunity, then we have the ability to alchemise our perspective (basic meaning: turning something from bad to good). By being conscious and aware of one's thought processes, we can transform what we know.

In this exercise I simply want you to take an objectified view of your current situation, think of something that you feel maybe is out of your control or a feeling of being overwhelmed. Now look at it from another perspective, instead of letting it consume you, take a step back, look at it from the outside looking in and then compare it to everything you have experienced in life. By doing this exercise you will realise that it is not so big, and you have the ability to look beyond it.

Notes:

CHAPTER SEVEN:

WISDOM

CROWN

Now we have reached the last chapter and the last Chakra. After checking your reality, making conscientious decisions, strengthening your willpower, thinking creatively and adapting transparent communication skills form a place of trust, you have been able to develop the Black Sheep mindset (whilst working through your Chakras).

In 2019 I had three jobs, I was still working full time (9-5), started my own business and was teaching yoga in the evenings. I knew something had to give, I was feeling burnt-out, exhausted and didn't have time to see the people or do the things I wanted. So I eventually quit my full time job (after being made redundant twice previously, I realised that I needed to take the leap and my own path, that the 9-5 corporate career wasn't for me) and decided to go all in with my business, to focus on the things that would ultimately make me happy. But I didn't just quit my job, I changed my lifestyle. I moved out of my beautiful apartment in Brighton with a sea view and moved abroad to Bali. To start my journey of being 100% all in. I knew I needed to make big change and it was the right time for me to do so (this was personal for me but this isn't for everyone. Small changes can also help your development and expansion).

Now, I am writing this chapter after being full circle around the world. I decided to write this last chapter from an ecological community, I wanted to experience what it was like to live completely off grid. Where the community make grow their own crops, build their own buildings, create their own water system and use solar panels to generate power (electricity). Honestly, I am completely out of my comfort zone, everything is very raw here and you definitely need to have an open mind to be able to adapt as there are no creature comforts. I step outside my Yurt and I am in the woods, surrounded by trees (it can be muddy and dirty). This is a self-build project, with no funding so everything is basic, and it will probably take a few more years to complete the project. However, it is refreshing to discover all the people living here have chosen their lifestyle and living through there authenticity. This of course is an extreme example but it shows that we all have the capability to create a life for ourselves away from the conditioning that we have been brought up to believe. All you need is faith in yourself to do so.

INNER REBEL

When we have broken the chains to what is holding us back, jumped over the fence from the pen we have been put in (cage or box), then we start to make decisions based on our own truth and reality. This gives us freedom and liberation to choose what is best for us and to make conscious decisions about our future, we act from a place of consciousness. So, does this really make us rebel or just a free thinker?

Your inner rebel wants to do what is right by you, even it means leaving the system behind and creating a new one, one of more value and purpose. That aligns with your authenticity and intuition. It can be said that being a rebel means to be conscious; awake and aware. Or it can be said to be destructive and wild. Maybe it means both, maybe we need to destroy to re-build. It is only when systems fall apart or break down that new ones are established.

Personally, I have always felt like the Black Sheep or rebel because I spoke up for injustice at work and freedom in life, when everyone else was silent. It is not easy because you initially receive a lot of judgment but after gain respect. This is why, having a strong core centre is necessary because it makes you resilient and unshakeable. It taught me that, unless I am working for a company that aligns with my values, then I would rather not work there. I have set-up several businesses and now mentoring others (being a trained lecturer). I wanted to lead from a place of authenticity and that meant setting up businesses that I felt passionate about, that gave me purpose and fulfilment (if you are reading this book then maybe you have had the same experience and looking to break the mould to re-build something from your essence).

AUTHENTICITY

Authenticity, generally speaking means truth or real. By saying something is authentic, it means it is genuine and normally of value. It can be described as the stamp that an artist or legal successor appends on the artwork or document. It can also be described as an antique or trademark, making it unique and one of a kind. This being said, when we come from a place of authenticity, we are also being unique and one of a kind (as there is no two people the same, not even twins or triplets). So once we align with our authenticity, we can bring something new and refreshing into the word.

Authenticity, when related to a person can be described as a conjunction of actions, values and beliefs. Living an authentic life has become increasing popular in today's culture because more people are acknowledging the old systems in place are no longer serving them and therefore striving for something that aligns with their values, creating a life of purpose. Acting with purpose creates the feeling of aligning you actions with the trueself.

Authenticity is a complex topic and can be hard to define, many philosophers have argued about the concept. Some stating that authenticity is something that is developed throughout life (knowing oneself) and others state it is always with us and it needs to be uncovered (like in the yoga philosophy, where it is said that we are born whole, it is the world that makes us feel not complete). In 2000, Michael Kernis and Brian Goldman developed their Authenticity Inventory, which simplified the concept and made it easier to digest. It comprised of four key factors: awareness, unbiased processing, behaviour, and relational orientation. All of which we have covered in this book, from creating awareness to questioning your reality. They all require introspection, analysing how we feel internally and examining on what is happening externally for us to feel and think this way. Then making proactive changes that align, taking authentic actions that align.

Once we have grasped this concept and start to put it into practice (remember this is a work in progress and we will probably need to come back and review several times, as growth is not linear, we are creating new neuro pathways) by living with authenticity then we can create a project or business that aligns. This then will make you feel more fulfilled because your beliefs and what you do aligns.

Authentic leadership is created by recognising how our neuro pathways communicate with one another, being straightforward, transparent, consistent and having a clear vision. The more we have clarity internally, the better we will be able to execute it. Therefore, bringing more clarity to each project for everyone involved. The more consistent the leader, the more trust is formed between the leader and the team, because the neuro pathways become stronger. For example, if someone always shows up and delivers, they gain trust. But if a leader is unreliable and contradicts themselves, the trust is fragmented and not so strong. Therefore being authentic, creates consistency because you know who you are and what you want, and with consistency, trust is built.

I think it is important to note what the word TRUST originally means; it means STRENGTH. The word trust comes from the Old Norse language and is translated from the word strength. As the Vikings raided and settled in new lands during the Viking Age, so too did their language. At its broadest extent, Old Norse was spoken in Scandinavia, Iceland, the Faroe Islands, the British Isles, continental Europe, Russia, Byzantium, Greenland, and even North America. Several common English words are loan words from Old Norse. When you hear the word trust, what do you think of? Most of the time we think of trust in relationship with others. But how about if you think of 'self-trust'. In order to be authentic, we need to establish self-trust which strengths our core and therefore strengthens our actions and relations with others.

The Authentic Leadership (2006) by Bill George is a relatively a new theory, that can be split up into three sections: Interpersonal Perspective, Developmental Processing and Relational Transparency. Each of these sections have their own meaning. Firstly, Interpersonal Perspective can be described as the leader's self-awareness, self-knowledge, self-regulation and self-concept. It is very much based on the leader perspective of themselves and their knowledge. Secondly,

Relational, this is how the leader relates to the team with transparency and clarity, building a trust framework. Thirdly, Developmental, bring a clear strategy that can be translated and maintained.

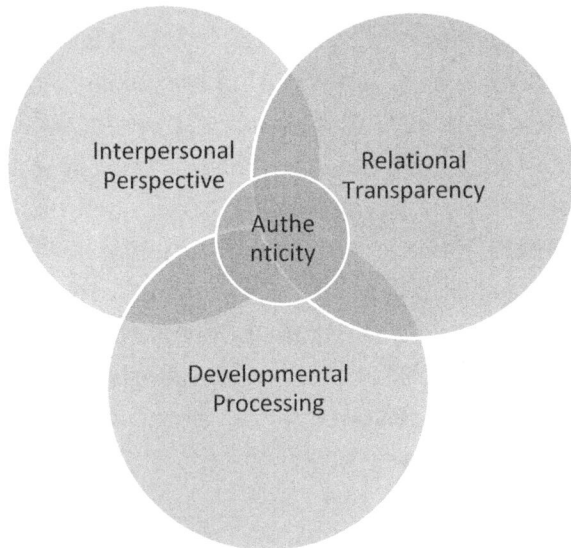

Interpersonal Perspective

Relational Transparency

Authe nticity

Developmental Processing

Bill George states that people in leadership roles lost the trust of their employees, customers and stakeholders and now only 18% of Americans trust the values and ethics of business leaders. He then continues to say that this has happened because we chose charismatic leaders, instead of character-based leaders. Valuing the image of the leader created a generation of psychopathic leaders, rather than leaders that practices integrity and deliver. This is where companies and businesses put style over substance and lost their core values.

This theory stems from the idea of 'being the example'. Changing, do as I say to do as I do. By putting words into actions and seeing them align, this is where trust can be built in leadership and business. Have you ever experienced this? I remember few years back, going for a promotion and the guy competing with me was very good at saying how good he was but in reality he did very little. Whereas I was very honest and humble. I didn't get the promotion and a few weeks later I resigned, I realised that I didn't want to work for a company that had a lack of values and that wasn't observing the employee's professionalism. I realised that I had become very drained in the role because I lacked purpose in my work and more importantly my values did clearly not align with the business framework. Ironically, when I handed in my resignation, I was offered a more senior role because the company realised they couldn't lose a hardworking and authentic employee. The fact I stood my ground and spoke my truth, made them value me (unfortunately it was too late, and I already made my mind up to leave). The fact is, the last generation have become very good at selling themselves but very little of them are original and genuine. We now have a generation that is narcissistic, portraying a external confidence but in reality have very little to offer. This is why the authentic leader is so necessary and is the new form of leadership, because they deliver and show up. They are true to themselves and therefore their customers, employees and colleagues. Which really does make all the difference.

"Don't strive for power over people, strive to empower the people" – Bill George

Authenticity is your trademark (yes, that's the name of the book) because being authentic is almost like an identity stamp or trademark. Being true to yourself and ignoring outside pressures from society makes to strong, sustainable and robust. Which ultimately builds good customer and employee relations because people know they can rely on you and you will not break in the storm. An authentic leader is a strong leader, they have built robust neuro pathways in their brain, therefore able to implement clarity through strong communication skills. It also makes you unique and different so you can stand out from the crowd in your marketplace. Giving you that extra **'je ne sais quoi'.**

WISDOM

Being authentic involves the ability to be introspective and understand what motivates oneself. This indeed requires wisdom. Bill George (2015) states that business leaders require emotional intelligence rather than academic intelligence. Highlighting the difference between knowledge and wisdom. Knowledge is a part of wisdom, but it means so much more. Wisdom is associated with character attributes such as unbiased judgment, compassion, experiential self-knowledge, self-transcendence and non-attachment, and virtues such as ethics and benevolence.

Wisdom can be slightly hard to define, as it is something we cannot see, it is a form of consciousness and the ability to be mindful. In many cultures it is suggested that we gain wisdom in adulthood, however, this has been argued with many psychologists and philosophers. Many philosophers have suggested that it has a spiritual element. Igor Grossmann (2017) suggests that wisdom involves a certain aspect of thinking (intellectual humility, recognition and uncertainty to change) which sounds very similar to the concept of authenticity. Grossmann suggests that an ego-decentring mind-set enables wise thinking and decision making. Which can be cognitive learning and development. Meaning that if you have an eco-decentring mind-set then you have the ability to disconnect and look at the bigger picture, with an objective view. That one can disconnect from an ideal or theoretical assumption of origin and make decisions based on accumulative facts and empathy. To not have a self-centred approach but detaching from the ego to create views and opinions from a place of wisdom.

If we analyse our thoughts and actions, then we can choose them more consciously and re-program our brain by using neuro plasticity (changing/re-programming our brain cells). The more we take conscious action steps, the more we can regulate our emotions and permanently change our brain, like a form of mental exercise. Being mind-full can also mean being wise, when we are mindful, we make conscientious decisions and actions. We become more present and aware, rather than mind-wondering.

By practising being wise and mindful then we can change our neuro pathways and make new connections in the brain by using neuro plasticity. Our brain changes in three ways when we practise mindfulness, it increases the Hippocampus and Temporal Parietal Junction but decreases Amygdala. Which means our memory and learning capability increases, our emotions regulate and we become more compassionate and empathetic. Whilst, becoming less stressed. As Amygdala is responsible for our fight or flight reaction so when this decreases so does our stress. We gain the ability to handle difficult situation and environments better because of the changes in our brain that happens through the transferal of chemical signals, changing the brain structure or enlarging parts and becoming more functional. The more we practice this, the more our brain regulates and builds robust neuro pathways, that gets stronger the more we do them.

If we release our ego; the vision we see of ourselves, that has been cast on us from culture conditioning (mentioned in chapters one, two and three). As the ego is not who we are but who we think we are because of what we have been told (or who we should be). So, if we release this vision of ourselves, we can connect to our true essence and authenticity. Which will enable us to make wise decisions and choices, in alignment with our true self. So, to conclude, to become wise, one needs to be awake, activating their neurons to create conscientious neuro pathways.

Only a Black Sheep can wake the sleeping sheep and lead the herd, bring them into a state of consciousness.

CROWN CHAKRA

Which brings us to the final Chakra in the sequence of seven, this Chakra is called the Crown. Crowns normally represent wisdom (the wise king or queen) and glory. This Chakra represents both wisdom and consciousness. Meaning being consciously awake and aware. At this stage our brain is fully active and our nervous system is balanced. Located at the top of the head; spiritually it is where we connect to a higher power, either source, divine, God or the Universe (what ever resonates with you). Physically it governs the central nervous system, pineal gland, pituitary gland, and skin. The pineal gland produces melatonin to affect the other glands in the endocrine system. When we have a healthy balance of the central nervous system we feel present with a sense of awareness. Everything we think, say and do will align with our authenticity. We will put our words into actions and see them manifest, by completing and achieving tasks, making wise decisions, creating clear connections and being innovative. It is when we are witnessing our best results.

Symptoms of imbalance:

Overactive	Underactive
Cynicism	Confusion
Attention Seeking	Disconnection
Apathy	Burnt-out

This can show-up in many forms, such as dizziness, migraines, chronic fatigue and hormonal imbalance. In order to avoid this then we need to neutralise our nervous system by paying attention to our patterns and habits, are we sleeping so we feel awake? Are we learning to activate our brain? Are the actions we are taking reflecting how we see ourselves?

By following the first Chakras we will create a sense of self, safety and purpose so we can lead with authenticity. Every great leader in history has been given a crown, the crown of wisdom and authenticity for every queen and king. Now wear yours!

EXERCISE 7: YOUR AUTHENTIC TRADEMARK

So, we come to the last exercise in the book as we come back to the root concept. Your authenticity, your inner rebel, the Black Sheep mindset. Ask yourself what sets you apart and embrace it! Being authentic fundamentally means being one of a kind, this is your trademark and what will make you like no other person or business in the market.

Look at your personal strengths and skills, what is your USP (unique selling point)? Then examine how they can be of service. Are you creative, empathetic, proactive etc? Is there a problem that you can solve by connecting with people or creating a new product? Your uniqueness is captivating and courageous.

Your Trademark:	Using my........to.........
Your USP	Your skills to be of service

Thank you for reading, the light that shines in me, shines in you.

Danielle X

Insta @holisticentrepreneurcoach

PS. If you need more work on one of the chapters, then I highly recommend doing more chakra work to unblock this area.

REFERENCE

Stella Collins, Neuroscience for Learning and Development: How to Apply Neuroscience and Psychology for Improved Learning and Training, 2nd ed. (London: Kogan Page, 2019).

Yoona Kang et al., "Effects of Self-Transcendence on Neural Responses to Persuasive Messages and Health Behavior Change," Proceedings of the National Academy of Sciences, Sept. 17, 2018, https://www.pnas.org/content/115/40/9974.

Collins, Neuroscience for Learning and Development.

Chip Heath and Dan Heath, Made to Stick: Why Some Ideas Survive and Others Die (New York: Random House, 2007).

Tim Herrera, "How to — Literally — Sound More Confident and Persuasive," Smarter Living, New York Times, Nov. 10, 2019, https://www.nytimes.com/2019/11/10/smarter-living/how-to-sound-more-confident-persuasive.html.

Michael L. Platt, The Leader's Brain Enhance Your Leadership, Build Stronger Teams, Make Better Decisions, and Inspire Greater Innovation with Neuroscience

Kirton, M. "Adaptors and innovators: a description and measure", Journal of Applied Psychology (61:5) 1976, pp 622–629.

Kirton, M.J. "Field Dependence and Adaptation Innovation Theories", Perceptual and Motor Skills, 1978, 47, pp 1239 1245.

Kirton, M.J. *Adaptation and innovation in the context of diversity and change* Routledge, London, 2003, p. 392

Levitt, Theodore (1986). The marketing imagination (New, expanded ed.). New York: Free Press.

"Unique Selling Proposition (USP)". Entrepreneur Europe. Retrieved 2020-03-29. Successful business ownership is not about having a unique product or service; it's about making your product stand out--even in a market filled with similar items.

Snyder, C. R., & Lopez, S. J. (2007). Positive psychology: The scientific and practical explorations of human strengths. Thousand Oaks, CA, US: Sage Publications

Jump up to:[a] [b] Lopez, S. J. (2006). "C. R. (Rick) Snyder (1944–2006)." American Psychologist, 61(7): 719.

Anton, Corey. Selfhood and Authenticity. Albany, NY: State University of New York Press, 2001.

Chen, Xunwu. Being and Authenticity. Value inquiry book series, v. 149. Amsterdam: Rodopi, 2004.

Ferrara, Alessandro, Reflective Authenticity: Rethinking the Project of Modernity, London and New York, Routledge, 1998. ISBN 041513062X

Golomb, Jacob. In Search of Authenticity From Kierkegaard to Camus. Problems of Modern European Thought. London: Routledge, 1995. ISBN 0415119464

Moore, Thomas. Original Self Living with Paradox and Authenticity. New York: HarperCollins, 2000. ISBN 0060195428

Nehamas, Alexander. Virtues of Authenticity Essays on Plato and Socrates. Princeton, N.J.: Princeton University Press, 1999. ISBN 0691001774

Taylor, Charles. The Ethics of Authenticity. Cambridge, Mass: Harvard University Press, 1992. ISBN 0674268636

Trilling, Lionel. Sincerity and Authenticity. Cambridge, Mass: Harvard University Press, 1972. ISBN 0674808606

Micheal H. Kernis. Brian M, Goldman. A Multicomponent Conceptualization of Authenticity: Theory and research
https://depts.washington.edu/uwcssc/sites/default/fil es/hw00/d40/uwcssc/sites/default/files/The%20Authe nticity%20Inventory.pdf

George, B. (2015). About Bill George. Retrieved from: http://www.billgeorge.org/page/about-bill-george

George, B. (2015). Harvard Life Hack: 5 Steps to Authentic Leadership with Bill George. Retrieved from: http://www.billgeorge.org/page/harvard-life-hack-5-steps-to-authentic-leadership-with-bill-george

Grossmann, I. (2017). "Wisdom in context". Perspectives on Psychological Science. 21 (12): 1254–1266. doi:10.1177/1745691616672066.

Sternberg, R. J. (1985). Implicit theories of intelligence, creativity, and wisdom. Journal of Personality and Social Psychology, 49, 607–62.

Walsh R. (June 2015). "What Is wisdom? Cross-cultural and cross-Disciplinary Syntheses". Review of General Psychology. 19 (3): 178–293. doi:10.1037/gpr0000045. S2CID 146383832.

Levitt, T (1983) The Marketing Imagination, New York: Free Press.

"Press Releases - News - Harvard Business School". www.hbs.edu. Retrieved 9 May 2019.

Jump up to:a b Mullman, Jeremy (July 10, 2006). "An 'original mind' of marketing dies". Advertising Age. 77: 8.

Levitt, Theodore (1 August 2002). "Creativity Is Not Enough". Retrieved 9 May 2019 – via hbr.org.

Levitt, Theodore (1 May 1981). "Marketing Intangible Products and Product Intangibles". Retrieved 9 May 2019 – via hbr.org.

Bowlby J (1999) [1969]. Attachment. Attachment and Loss (vol. 1) (2nd ed.). New York: Basic Books.

Bowlby J (1973). Separation: Anxiety & Anger. Attachment and Loss (vol. 2); (International psycho-analytical library no.95). London: Hogarth Press.

Bowlby J (1980). Loss: Sadness & Depression. Attachment and Loss (vol. 3); (International psycho-analytical library no.109). London: Hogarth Press.

Bowlby J (1988). A Secure Base: Parent-Child Attachment and Healthy Human Development. Tavistock professional book. London: Routledge.

Seeman, M. (1966). Status and identity: The problem of inauthenticity. The Pacific Sociological Review, 9 (2), 67–73.

George, B. (2003). Authentic leadership: Rediscovering the secrets to creating lasting value. San Francisco: Jossey-Bass.

Jump up to:a b George, B., & Sims, P. (2007). True north: Discover your authentic leadership. San Francisco: Jossey-Bass.

Luthans, F., & Avolio, B. J. (2003). Authentic leadership development. In K. S. Cameron, J. E. Dutton, & R. E. Quinn (Eds.), Positive organizational scholarship: Foundations of a new discipline (pp. 241–261). San Francisco: Barrett-Koehler.

Jump up to:[a] [b] [c] Walumbwa, F. O., Avolio, B. J., Gardner, W. L., Wernsing, T. S., & Peterson, S. J. (2008). Authentic leadership: Development and validation of a theory-based measure. Journal of Management, 34, 89–126.

Printed in Great Britain
by Amazon